The Development of Profes Management

This shortform book presents key peer-reviewed research selected by expert series editors and contextualised by new analysis from each author on the development of professional management.

With contributions on consultancy and the training of consultants, Taylorism and its appeal to socialists, the social position of managers, and the growth of the managerial class, this volume provides an array of fascinating insights into industrial history.

Of interest to business and economic historians, this shortform book also provides analysis and illustrative case studies that will be valuable reading across the social sciences.

John F. Wilson is Pro Vice-Chancellor (Business and Law) at Northumbria University, Newcastle. He has published widely in the fields of business, management, and industrial history, including ten monographs, six edited collections, and over seventy articles and chapters.

Ian Jones is a Senior Research Assistant at Newcastle Business School, Northumbria University, and won the John F. Mee Best Paper Award at the Academy of Management in 2018 for his contribution to the Management History Division.

Steven Toms is Professor of Accounting at the University of Leeds. He is a former editor of *Business History*. His research interests are focused on accounting and financial history and the history of the textile industry.

Routledge Focus on Industrial History
Series Editors: John F. Wilson, Steven Toms and Ian Jones

This shortform series presents key peer-reviewed research originally published in the *Journal of Industrial History*, selected by expert series editors and contextualised by new analysis from each author on how the specific field addressed has evolved.

Of interest to business historians, economic historians and social scientists interested in the development of key industries, the series makes theoretical and conceptual contributions to the field, as well as providing a plethora of empirical, illustrative and detailed case-studies of industrial developments in Britain, the United States and other international settings.

A Search for Competitive Advantage
Case Studies in Industrial History
Edited by John F. Wilson, Steven Toms and Ian Jones

Knowledge Management
Dependency, Creation and Loss in Industrial History
Edited by John F. Wilson, Ian Jones and Steven Toms

The Development of Professional Management
Training, Consultancy, and Management Theory
in Industrial History
Edited by John F. Wilson, Ian Jones and Steven Toms

For more information about this series, please visit: www.routledge.com/Routledge-Focus-on-Industrial-History/book-series/RFIH

The Development of Professional Management

Training, Consultancy, and Management Theory in Industrial History

Edited by
John F. Wilson, Ian Jones,
and Steven Toms

Routledge
Taylor & Francis Group
LONDON AND NEW YORK

First published 2022
by Routledge
2 Park Square, Milton Park, Abingdon, Oxon OX14 4RN

and by Routledge
605 Third Avenue, New York, NY 10158

Routledge is an imprint of the Taylor & Francis Group, an informa business

British Library Cataloguing-in-Publication Data
A catalogue record for this book is available from the British Library

Library of Congress Cataloging-in-Publication Data
Names: Wilson, J. F., editor. | Jones, Ian (Senior research assistant), editor. | Toms, Steven, editor.
Title: The development of professional management : training, consultancy, and management theory in industrial history / edited by John F. Wilson, Ian Jones and Steven Toms.
Description: Abingdon, Oxon ; New York, NY : Routledge, 2022. | Series: Routledge focus on industrial history | Includes bibliographical references and index.
Identifiers: LCCN 2021014105 (print) | LCCN 2021014106 (ebook)
Subjects: LCSH: Management--Social aspects. | Industrial management--History. | Consultants.
Classification: LCC HD31.2 .D47 2022 (print) | LCC HD31.2 (ebook) | DDC 658.4/07124--dc23
LC record available at https://lccn.loc.gov/2021014105
LC ebook record available at https://lccn.loc.gov/2021014106

ISBN: 978-1-032-03840-7 (hbk)
ISBN: 978-1-032-07453-5 (pbk)
ISBN: 978-1-003-20699-6 (ebk)

DOI: 10.4324/9781003206996

Typeset in Times New Roman
by codeMantra

Contents

List of contributors   vii

Introduction   1

**1 Models of management education and training:
   the 'Consultancy Approach'**   5
   MICHAEL FERGUSON

**2 Visible hands and visible handles: understanding the
   managerial revolution in the UK**   40
   JOHN QUAIL

**3 The evolution of education and training in
   British management consultancy**   66
   MICHAEL FERGUSON

**4 Marxist manager amidst the Progressives:
   Walter N. Polakov and the Taylor Society**   96
   DIANA KELLY

Retrospective   116
   DIANA KELLY

Index   119

Contributors

Michael Ferguson completed his PhD thesis at the Open University in 2000 titled *The Origin, Gestation, and Evolution of Management Consultancy Within Britain (1869–1965): The Principles, Practices, and Techniques of a New Professional Grouping.*

Diana Kelly has worked at the University of Wollongong in various roles since 1983 and is currently an Associate Professor in the School of Humanities and Social Inquiry. She has researched and published on topics such as workplace bullying, industrial relations, the history of business and management thought, and women in history. She has recently published a book titled *The Red Taylorist: The Life and Works of Walter Nicholas Polokav* (2020).

John Quail received his external doctorate in business history from Leeds University in 1996. He has never held an academic post, not for the want of trying, but applications for first academic posts when you are the same age as the head of department will never go very well. He has contributed to a number of business history journals and edited compilations. In retirement he has been appointed a Visiting Fellow in York Management School.

Introduction

Purpose and significance of the series

Routledge Focus on Industrial History is a shortform book series motivated by the desire to provide an outlet for articles originally published in the defunct *Journal of Industrial History* (*JIH*). By using an extensive repository of top-quality publications, the series ensures that the authors' findings contribute to recent debates in the field of management and industrial history. Indeed, the articles contained in these volumes will appeal to business historians, economic historians and social scientists interested in longitudinal studies of the development of key industries and themes. Moreover, the series will provide fresh insight into how the academic field has developed over the past twenty years.

The original peer-reviewed articles are built on robust business-historical research methodologies and are subject to extensive primary research. The series provides a plethora of empirical, illustrative and detailed case studies of industrial developments in the United Kingdom, the United States and other international settings.

Building on the original *Journal of Industrial History*

The first edition of the *Journal of Industrial History* was published in 1998, with the aim of providing 'clear definitional parameters for industrial historians' and in turn establishing links between 'industrial history and theoretical work in social science disciplines like economics, management (including international business), political science, sociology, and anthropology'. Because it has been more than twenty years since its original publication, it is clear that the relevance of the *JIH* has stood the test of time. The original *JIH* volumes covered a diverse range of topics, including industrial structure and behaviour,

DOI: 10.4324/9781003206996

especially in manufacturing and services; industrial and business case studies; business strategy and structure; nationalisation and privatisation; globalisation and competitive advantage; business culture and industrial development; education, training and human resources; industrial relations and its institutions; the relationship between financial institutions and industry; industrial politics, including the formulation and impact of industrial and commercial policy; and industry and technology.

Volume eight: contribution and key findings

The eighth volume of this series focuses on the development of professional management in industrial history. This volume examines a broad range of developments within the field of management in Britain and the United States. The articles in this volume show the development of training systems for professional management, the role of consultants in the development of professional management and the impact of management theory on a variety of political ideologies.

The first chapter, 'Models of management education and training: the "consultancy approach"' by Michael Ferguson, argues for greater recognition of the role of consultants and consultancy firms in the training and professionalisation of management in Britain during the twentieth century. This chapter documents the development of the consultancy profession from the mid- to late nineteenth century and throughout the twentieth century, moving from consultants operating on-site to improve operating procedures and train managers in their implementation and use, to more specialised off-site training for mangers, greater specialisation of consultants as new industries developed post-Second World War, to the mixed approach of consultancy firms today. This chapter not only shows the importance of consultants in developing management capabilities, but also shows the development of consultants themselves over time, from experienced generalists to educated specialists, as well as the development of professional bodies that aim to establish standardised approaches to consulting and industry-accepted certification.

The second chapter, 'Visible hand and invisible handles: understanding the managerial revolution in the UK' by John Quail, seeks to understand what drove the managerial revolution in Britain during the twentieth century. Quail reviews four possible explanations for the managerial revolution in Britain from a variety of intellectual traditions: arguments from Bruno Rizzi and James Burnham that the managerial revolution is the product of a revolutionary managerial class that will lead to post-capitalist, post-democratic managed societies; the arguments of Adolf Berle and Gardiner Means that the managerial revolution was a natural result of the separation between ownership and control; Alfred Chandler Jr's argument that it was a triumph of managerial coordination over market coordination in large US companies; and arguments put forward by Chandler, Jean-Jacques Servan-Schreiber and Harold Perkin who state that the managerial revolution in the United States created a competitive advantage for those firms who could adapt their organisational structure to take advantage of it, necessitating competitors in Britain and Europe to follow. Quail critiques these arguments and their applicability to Britain, instead, suggesting a fifth argument of his own. Inspired by the work of Michel Foucault, Quail argues that the lateness of the managerial revolution in Britain can be attributed to the need for British companies to develop excess managerial capacity in order to adapt to the market conditions they were facing.

The third chapter, 'The evolution of education and training in British management consultancy' by Michael Ferguson, builds on his earlier work on consultancy in Britain, expanding his analysis of the development of the consultancy industry and the training of consultants. This chapter shows four periods in the twentieth century that characterise the methods of training for consultants. This chapter shows the changes in scale and scope of the consultancy industry necessitating changes in the methods of educating new consultants into the field. Moving from individual, on-site training in the early twentieth century, off-site class-based training became the norm as the demand for qualified consultants outstripped the supply and the ability of previous methods to train consultants fast enough. As the new industries developed that required specialised knowledge, consultancy firms adjusted by increasingly relying on workers with academic qualifications as a prerequisite rather than industry experience, allowing for training to be tailored to industry needs. This chapter takes us up to the end of the twentieth century with the mixed approach often being adopted, with academic qualifications still relevant, but with digital technology allowing for new methods of dissemination and training allowing for consultants to be rapidly trained as jobs require rather than specialising in particular industries.

The final chapter, 'Marxist manager amidst the progressives: Walter N. Polakov and the Taylor Society' by Diana Kelly, shows how the Taylorism held appeal to people from vastly different ideological positions through the work of Walter Polakov and his membership of the Taylor Society. Polakov, a committed socialist and skilled engineer, saw Taylorism as a way of ensuring society could benefit from the greater efficiency of labour and creating easier work rather than as a method of controlling employees. Arguing that capitalism was the main driver of inefficiencies, Polakov argued that not only was efficiency of production a public good, but that Taylorism would enable workers to show the value of their labour in productive processes, allowing for a fair distribution of wages based on the value added by labour. This chapter shows that the development of management theory was of interest to more than just those who wished to make existing systems work more efficiently in pursuit of greater profits for owners.

Conclusion

It is apparent from this brief review of the chapter that the eighth volume in the series makes important contributions to the field of industrial history in several ways. First, it provides a series of high calibre and unique studies in aspects of industrial history that contribute to more recent debates on the development of professional management, the role of consultancy in the development of professional management in Britain, and the appeal and use of scientific management principles. Second, the chapters shed light on the broader subjects of societal views on education and academic qualifications in business, the social position of management and forces that enable or prohibit the development of the managerial classes. Finally, this volume provides strong historical case studies that can be used by students and researchers who are exploring issues related to the development of professional management in Britain and the United States. The editors believe that this volume will not only provide a much wider audience for articles that link into a range of topical issues but also feed into debates in the wider social sciences. These are themes that will be demonstrated in previous volumes in the *Routledge Series of Industrial History*, highlighting the intrinsic value in republishing material from the *Journal of Industrial History* and ensuring that the articles contribute extensively to current debates.

1 Models of management education and training

The 'Consultancy Approach'*

Michael Ferguson

The long term objective of all management consultancy is education. The only complete management consulting job is the management consulting job that leaves the client's managerial staff re-educated, alive, educating themselves.[1]

In 1986, the National Economic Development Council, the Manpower Commission and the British Institute of Management together sponsored research into management education and training. The purpose of the research was to examine what was going on within competitor countries as a comparator with the provision of management education and training in Britain at that time. The competitor countries reviewed were the United States, Japan, France and West Germany, with the output of the research being an official publication entitled 'The Making of Managers'.[2] The information obtained through the research was subsequently published in a book in 1988 under the title 'Making Managers'.[3] Within the book, each of the countries was examined in turn. As far as the British experience was concerned, the author of the chapter, Charles Handy, developed the notion that there were three models of management education and training: the 'Corporate Approach', the 'Academic Approach' and the 'Professional Approach'.[4] The findings of both the report (official publication) and the subsequent book related to the situation that existed by the mid-1980s. There was no attempt to map the progression of management education and training within Britain, other than through a short historical sketch of some of the main events that had occurred within these fields. The purpose of this article is not to challenge the notion of models or the situation described within both documents in relation to the mid-1980s. The purpose is to put forward the position that there was a fourth model, the 'Consultancy Approach'. This model was both inextricably linked with the historical situation of the other three and important, in its own right, with regard to the

DOI: 10.4324/9781003206996-1

progression of management education and training in Britain in the twentieth century.[5] In addition, this article will indicate that the progression of management education and training, certainly with regard to the Consultancy Approach, is linked with the notion that management was not a subject for which a formal occupational education was applicable. It was only through changes to this dominant position over time that the peculiar situation within Britain with regard to the education and training of managers evolved more positively.

In order to provide a coherent argument, this article is broken down into a number of sections. The first section examines in outline the historical progression of management education and training in Britain during the twentieth century through to the period preceding the time frame concerned with 'The Making of Managers' study. Handy's findings, specifically the make-up of his three models, are examined in the second section. The third section examines the input of the management consultant through two distinct forms of role: the 'Direct' and 'Indirect' roles. The difference between the two largely relates to their immediacy of impact. There is then a conclusion that attempts to bring together the various themes and highlight the notion that there was in fact a fourth model of education and training, the Consultancy Approach. This is achieved through reviewing Handy's three models and the work of the consultants. This review will highlight that not only was the Consultancy Approach distinctive in its own right, but that elements of it were present in each of the other three models.

I. Management education and training in the twentieth century to the 1980s

The development of management education and training, encompassing all inputs into the process of improvement through both direct and indirect instructions, was not a dynamic process in the first half of the twentieth century. Keeble charts this lack of progress, describing a grim situation in which the only available avenue for continuing education was 'after-work study'.[6] Such an education could be obtained through the mix of courses on offer at the technical schools, leading to a multiplicity of qualifications, or through the universities where courses were on offer at degree and pre-degree level. This may be a general statement of the situation, but it does, nonetheless, provide a backdrop for developing an understanding of what was going on up to that time. Ultimately, she describes an un-coordinated approach nationally, with the ability to choose a defined path to assist in career development hampered by an ad hoc array of courses with no defined progressive output.[7] However, she does qualify this statement, somewhat, by stating that 'Many (institutions) offered courses leading to qualifications of (some of) the professional institutes'.[8] The point being made here was that there was a common element, 'management', but this element was treated differently, by and large, by the various bodies and providers. However, obtaining such qualifications was hampered by the necessity to acquire them in a manner that provided an additional burden for the student. 'They studied for them outside of working hours – via correspondence courses, or evening classes in schools, technical colleges, and universities'.[9] Having said this, this particular regime of training may not have been totally unwelcome by businesses at that time as it was both relatively costless to them and it enabled an identification of those individuals who were demonstrating a willingness to improve their employability and knowledge.

The 1945 General Election witnessed the arrival of a new Labour Government with a large majority following a campaign that was dominated by the concept of full employment.[10] The primary objectives of the government were rooted in the experiences of the past, specifically the unemployment situation of the 1930s.[11] Consequently, the Government's objectives were centred on the birth of the Welfare State that had as its central feature the National Health Service. In addition, the nationalisation of major industries and services, including coal mining, railways and the major utilities, was a central tenet of government policy. In support of the government's aims, there was an emphasis on industrial productivity. Three major initiatives were launched in the immediate post-war period:

1   The Privy Council Committee on Industrial Productivity, which had as its chairman Sir Henry Tizard. This was set up in December 1947 to find the ways and means for the government to improve industrial productivity.
2   An approach to the United States Economic Co-operation Administration, the body that administered Marshall Aid (European reconstruction), that led to the establishment of the Anglo American Productivity Council in 1947.
3   The 1944 Education Act, implemented in 1948, raised the compulsory school leaving age to fifteen. This resulted in a general raising of the standard of education and prevented young people from entering the labour market for a further year.

The first two initiatives were concerned with management, a subject that was beginning to take centre stage in the Government's concerns.[12]

In parallel with those initiatives, and immediately before them, two further initiatory movements were in train. The first of these was the Ministry of Education (Urwick) Committee on education for management. The purpose of the Committee was to advise the Minister on the requirements to initiate training for managers. This had organisation studies as a particular emphasis.[13] The second movement was the formation of the Baillieu Committee to advise on the creation of a central institute of management. Government had already made up its mind that a central institution would be formed and that a programme of management education would take place; the purpose of both committees was to detail how those initiatives would be implemented. However, these initiatives were not interrelated and this was a weakness in the whole approach. At the same time, in the post-war period, much the same as in the interwar era, the general situation remained. There still existed confusion in terms of a clearly defined and universally recognised progressive route for management education and training. Once again, this was reflected in an ad hoc array of courses available within both technical schools and universities, resulting in a wide range of qualifications, with no clearly defined path or focus in terms of management. This situation was confirmed by Silberston, who considered that the majority of courses on offer contained subjects that were only loosely related to the field of management, a point made by Handy in the following section.[14] Within such courses, with the exception of the Certificate and Diploma in Management Studies, later revised in 1961, the subject of management was not the central theme.[15] For example, at university level, the Commerce degree tended to be the main course, with management as a subject effectively being relegated to modular status within the overall course structure. As an aside, the base literature for these higher-level education courses at that time tended to have originated in the United States. This was because whilst there was a growing literature base in this country, the majority of books were written for a business audience. In other words, in the main, they were practical guides for improvement rather than meeting the exacting academic standards required for use in the universities and other educational institutes. They were, however, used quite extensively within the Certificate and Diploma courses in the technical and commercial colleges.

A more detailed review of the post-war situation supports the generalised contention described above, because while there were movements within academic circles and a recognition of the need for developing an educational platform for managers, this was hampered by attitudes both within businesses and academia in general. For example, many within business either believed that management was a practical subject that could only be learnt on the job, partly steeped within the tradition of 'managers are born, not made', or that it was a subject that could not be defined and taught.[16] To that end, it was argued that the ability to manage was an in-bred quality and individuals simply required some form of 'grooming' to make them effective within the firm. Within academia, a similar situation occurred in that, according to Wilson, academics were slow to take up the opportunities afforded by developments within management itself.[17] This was with the exception of those involved in the formation of the Foundation for Management Education in 1960.[18] This catastrophic combination meant that Britain was not on a progressive path to developing a definitive solution for the education and training needs of Britain's managers.[19]

This fragmented situation is confirmed within a series of publications produced by the British Institute of Management (BIM), variously titled but generally known as 'A Conspectus of Management Education'.[20] The first edition stated: 'The majority of courses included can probably be regarded as on the borders of management'.[21] This confirms Silberston's contention, quoted earlier.[22] Adopting the presentation structure within this series of publications, a review of the university courses reveals that even up until the publication of the fifth edition in 1963 the majority of courses at undergraduate level had only tenuous links with management or business. They were concerned with subjects such as business administration, commerce, social science and economics, with the subject of management modularised within them.[23] However, in terms of postgraduate courses, extra mural and miscellaneous courses, even within the second edition in 1955, various part-time courses and seminars started appearing with the word management within their titles, albeit they were few and far between.[24] These increased in numbers through time, with courses in functional management areas, techniques and general management providing the mainstay of the course types on offer within this broad subject area. By the time of the 1968 edition, it was becoming commonplace within universities to see the titles such as 'School of Management', 'Centre for Management Studies', 'Department of Industrial Administration' or 'Department of Business Studies' within university organisations.[25] This may have reflected a more serious approach to the delivery of educational courses in the fields of business and management. This was supported by the increased prominence of instances of postgraduate and diploma courses in management subjects across the range of universities within Britain. Just prior to this, in 1965 the Council for Academic Awards was formed to encourage polytechnics and other colleges to take up first degrees in business and management studies, providing them with equivalent status to university colleges. However, having said this, the numbers of courses were relatively few when compared with today's figures.

In further education (technical and commercial colleges, and colleges of further education), the mainstay of the curriculars in general throughout the period covered by 'The Conspectus' series of booklets was a combination of:

1   British Institute of Management and Ministry of Education Certificate and Diploma in Management Studies (changing to the Diploma in Management of Studies when it replaced the aforementioned qualifications),[26] and

2   Management modules for the qualifications of the professional institutes and associations.

However, increasingly throughout the whole period covered by the BIM series of publications, various short courses, programmes and seminars in management appeared within the curriculars of the array of further education colleges in Britain. They ranged in duration from a matter of days to weeks and months, the majority offering no formal qualifications, and were generally either full-time, part-time, sandwich or block release type courses. These were classified by the BIM as courses in either general management, functional management, management techniques, management skills or background courses. The majority of courses, even within the final edition of the BIM series, were either in functional management or in functional techniques, with the incidence of general management courses rising slowly over time, but representing only a small fraction of the total number of courses.[27] Within the private training sector, the few institutions that delivered training for managers fell within the same trap of delivering an ad hoc array of courses, largely with a practical content. The volume of these institutions grew slowly in numbers throughout the post-war period, but the delivery of courses in general management subjects was by and large the preserve of the Administrative Staff College at Henley and some, notably Urwick, Orr and Partners Ltd, management consultant company training schools.[28]

What 'The Conspectus' series of booklets confirmed throughout their existence was the observations of commentators that had reviewed the education and training situation within Britain in the post-war period. The lack of co-ordination across the range of providers failed to lead to a defined progressive path, with the overwhelming majority of courses receiving no formal recognition or qualification universally. One would be forgiven for thinking that the formation of the two business schools in London and Manchester in the mid-1960s, the increased interest in education and training for management by the academic and business communities, together with some in government, and the rising number of courses on offer across the range of providers would act as a light for shining the way forward. In many respects, this had the opposite effect, confirming Handy's summation of the situation in the mid-1980s (discussed in the next section). This is exemplified by the situation in the mid-1970s in which the 'duopoly' of London and Manchester in the delivery of postgraduate courses in business administration had been eroded through competition from other educational institutes.[29] Not only did competition alone cause confusion, but variations in length of course and content further exacerbated the situation. Therefore, a defined approach and structure to management education and training in Britain was still some way off. However, all of this has not taken account of the company-specific approach to the training of managers in Britain's industrial and commercial organisations. This issue is raised by Handy in the next section, in which he identifies three distinct Approaches, or models, extant within the mid-1980s.

II. The making of managers

The purpose of the study and subsequent book, described initially within the introduction to this article, was to examine what was going on within competitor countries as a comparator with the provision of management education and training in Britain at that time (mid-1980s).[30] The consequential outcome of the research enabled similarities and differences to be identified and to make recommendations, at a high level, on the approach Britain could take into the future to provide a structured and recognised approach to the progression of management through a regime of education and training. However, important as these aspects are, this article is more concerned with the models of education and training developed by Handy in Chapter 6 of the book and reviewing these in the light of historical research into the work of management consultants in Britain. The three models developed by Handy, the Corporate, Professional and Academic Approaches, encompassed the whole range of delivery within the fields of management education and training in Britain at the point of the mid-1980s. Because there was no attempt to chart the historical foundations of each, then the overall involvement of consultants in their progression has not been described. It is consequently essential, firstly, to provide the foundations for assisting our understanding of the work of consultants in the educational and training fields, before going on to clarify the role consultants had played in the development of British management education and training.[31]

Handy suggested that the lack of structure and progression in the development of British managers partly owed itself to the relatively low status historically attached to the title manager. This is because the term manager was used to describe a role within a functional area of the firm, for example transport manager, whereas strategic decision-making was the concern of principals, partners, directors or even permanent secretaries. At the same time, Handy noted that a career in business was viewed by many as a lowly occupation.[32] This situation began to be reversed in the post-Second World War period. However, the legacy remained with education and training in management progressing at a slower pace in this country in comparison with others abroad.[33] In parallel with this, another peculiarity of the British experience was the growth in the number of professional associations and institutes. These covered a range of occupations 'whose work requires some understanding of business or management and who therefore make some knowledge or experience of this a part of their qualifications'.[34] Therefore, it should come as no surprise that one of the Approaches to education and training identified by Handy was the Professional Approach.

The Professional Approach is a descriptor of a methodology that enabled individuals to 'earn while they learned'. In general terms, it is 'a mixture of tutored work experience (articles) with formal study leading to a graded series of qualifications, normally ending with membership of an institution'.[35] For those with occupations outside of the general management field, such education and training consisted of modules or aspects of management and business within the general framework of the occupational qualification. However, there are advantages and disadvantages with this type of approach to management development. Certainly within the confines of the professional qualifications, there is a structured and standard approach to learning. On the other hand, the qualifications cannot be easily fitted in with a wider portfolio of management qualifications, as in the majority of cases management is not the core subject. Equally, because each profession views the competences of business and management differently from an occupational perspective, there is little or no standardisation between individual professional approaches. At the same time, not all those who have an involvement in management are members of professional institutes or hold professional qualifications. This may partly explain why Handy felt it necessary to mention that:

> there is also a distrust of professional bodies who are often regarded as closed shop monopolies, protected by law from competition and therefore slow to change. The privileged position of many of the bodies makes their examinations, courses and membership procedures attractive to the young, but not always to employers.[36]

However, the Professional Approach, with its relatively long tradition, provides for an explanation of only one model. The next model, the Corporate Approach, is a description of the training conducted within a business for a business. It is an insular model of training delivery.

The Corporate Approach, in simple terms, is a method of staff training to meet the business needs of the organisation. According to Handy, management recruits were generally identified and recruited from polytechnics and universities. Within this general model, individuals were trained to meet the immediate functional requirements of their roles. Therefore, training and experience were normally geared towards a long-term career within the firm. This tended to be job specific, because a move towards a general management appointment was viewed as an occurrence that took place later within an individual's career when a broader approach to management training was adopted. However, this training delivery form was, primarily, only usual within larger organisations that had their own training departments – more recently (for example, in the 1980s) management consultant companies supplemented in-house training programmes.[37] The primary advantage of this approach was that firms trained their personnel towards the needs and goals of the organisation, and not for any wider application of management or management qualification. The disadvantages are clearly related to the lack of transferable knowledge, because of the firm-centred approach to training and the lack of formally recognised qualifications.

The final model, the Academic Approach, was viewed by Handy as being a replication of the American form of business education, with a jungle of courses in a range of qualifications taught at different levels across the whole academic community. In the mid-1980s, the situation was confusing because of the individual's inability to chart a clearly defined path through the range of qualifications and courses.[38] While the main advantage of this approach is clearly related to the achievement of formal qualifications, even in the mid-1980s universal recognition of some of these qualifications was still conspicuous by its absence. The two principal disadvantages of this approach related to the quality of teaching and the remoteness of the content of the courses from the practical setting. In terms of the quality of teaching, Handy described a spectrum, with good and bad at each end of the scale. The main problem with quality was that it was not visible to employers – they had no way in which to judge a good course from a bad course. This was exacerbated through a general shortage of good quality teachers and the lack of practitioner involvement in their delivery. In terms of content, there was a view that much of it was irrelevant, 'ignoring the practical and personal competences, of creating exaggerated ambitions in the minds of their students and of reductionism, of reducing the complexities of management to over-simple rules and principles'.[39]

In general terms, Handy suggested that the whole spectrum of management education and training within Britain was un-coordinated and difficult to subsume into a general model. This view of an un-coordinated and ad hoc approach nationally to management education and training is supported by the historical context described in the previous section. However, the input of consultants has suffered from a lack of recognition, both within historical descriptions of the situation and in Handy's review. This next section addresses this deficiency and places the work of management consultants in the historical context. This will provide the necessary building blocks for the creation of the fourth model of management education and training, the Consultancy Approach, described in the final section of this article.

III. The input of the consultants

The first section of this article described in outline what had been going on within the fields of management education and training up to the 1970s and 1980s. The second section provided a descriptive account of Handy's three models, which in effect reflected the British situation in the 1980s. Both these sections provide the necessary background information to put into perspective the work of management consultants, of which little has been reported on in the past. The quotation at the beginning of this article helps to describe the philosophical approach adopted by many of the management consulting companies, at least for the first half of the twentieth century.[40] Therefore, because of this, it is not surprising that the history of management consulting in Britain (from at least 1869) is littered with countless examples of the involvement of management consultants in the fields of management education, training and development.[41] The purpose of this section of the article is to describe that involvement and identify the various aspects of the general approach adopted by them throughout their history to the period of the 1980s. In broad-brush terms, two forms of delivery mechanisms were utilised by consultants in the dissemination of knowledge towards the objective of providing services in education and training for managers. These mechanisms are best understood from the perspective of two distinct roles:

Direct Role: Training delivered as part of an assignment or through formal training courses (either at the client's premise or at a training school), the provision of tuition through correspondence courses and assistance provided to companies in setting up their own training operations. Importantly, coaching by consultants during the course of an assignment was the dominant feature of on-site direct training during the whole period to at least the mid-1960s. Included within this general role is the work carried out by consultants within the professionalisation process of various occupations and assistance to educational institutions in the furtherance of their programmes.

Indirect Role: Knowledge provided through the delivery of lectures to professional and other forms of groups, and through publications of various types. In addition, it will be shown that the work of consultants was continued either deliberately or through imitation at the conclusion of assignments, and this represents another form of indirect input.

In order to develop an understanding of the roles, and the way in which they fitted in with the general working practices of the consultancy companies, a short historical digression will help paint the scene. In general terms, the management consultancy environment in Britain during the period 1869–1925 was dominated by a small number of sole practitioners. These men largely delivered services in the areas of production efficiency and/or costing, although there are a few early examples of work carried out in sales management and the development of management information processes.[42] In 1926, the first organised consultancy company commenced operations in Britain – Charles E. Bedaux and Company.[43] This was a subsidiary of the Bedaux organisation that had been founded in the United States in the second decade of the century. The Bedaux company delivered services in the areas of production efficiency and labour cost control. Three years later (1929), Harold Whitehead and Staff was formed for the express purpose of delivering sales training to the gas industry, with its first client being the

British Commercial Gas Association (BCGA).[44] The company widened its approach and provided consultancy services in sales management, sales staff training and retail management, although data on clients and the exact number of assignments carried out in these fields have not survived until the present day.[45] In 1934, two further British management consulting companies were formed, Production Engineering (now part of Lorien Consulting) and Urwick, Orr and Partners, largely concerning themselves with a similar range of services to the Bedaux company, but with refinements to methodology, and breadth of service delivery and approach. In addition, both these companies expressed the intention of expanding their service range into all areas in a client organisation where management had an interest. This was a change in philosophical stance, because to that point in time consultants were only involved in improvements to shop floor operational efficiency. The final major consultancy company formed within this period was Personnel Administration in 1943 (now known as PA Consulting Group), initially starting up as an operational training consultancy, primarily delivering operator training.[46] These companies, with the exception of Harold Whitehead and Partners, dominated the British management consultancy scene until the end of the 1960s.[47] They were generally known as the 'Big Four', delivering about three-quarters of all consultant services in Britain during the period 1930–1960s.[48] However, in the immediate post-war period a number of important firms were formed, for example the Anne Shaw Organisation in 1945 that specialised in motion study assignments and Harold Norcross and Partners whose services were largely concerned with production efficiency.[49]

The range of services provided by management consultant companies and sole practitioners, with minor exceptions, to the Second World War was concentrated in the functional (operational) areas of client firms, either within the production or administration departments. During the war, in addition to their main concentration in the area of production efficiency, consultants were engaged in the work of government departments, in planning assignments and delivering services in operator training. The post-war period witnessed a boom in services in support of improving productivity and the embryonic beginnings of services in a range of management areas. The balance between the two forms of general service area shifted significantly from the period of the mid- to late 1960s towards services in support of the management objective. Additionally, in the post-war period a number of small consultancies and partnerships were formed, largely concerned with specialised service delivery. At the same time, some of the major accountancy companies began to form their own consulting arms, while by the 1960s and 1970s a small number of major American consulting companies had set up operations in this country. The post-war period progressively witnessed a switch in emphasis in terms of the type of services delivered by consultancies, reflected in a movement away from productivity services towards services directed at the management functions and at boardroom level. To a large extent, the consultants' involvement in management education and training mirrored this changing environment in terms of subject matter.

The story of the involvement of management consultants in management education and training commences, in some small way, with the first known recorded incidence of management consulting assignments in the mid- to late 1860s. This individual was Montague Whitmore, a chartered accountant, of Clerkenwell Green, London, who employed techniques in costing and management accounting.[50] While little is known of the activities of these early consultant pioneers, and Whitmore is no exception, there are indications that they put in place processes and methods for the continuance of their recommendations following the conclusion of their assignments.[51] However, in terms of the orientation with regard to their inputs into management education and training, the majority fell within the area of the Indirect Role in terms of the delivery of lectures and the writing of papers in technical and professional journals. However, probably the most well-known consultant during that early period at the end of the nineteenth and beginning of the twentieth centuries was Alexander Hamilton Church. Church was a prolific writer of papers and advocate of standard costing methodologies. It was written of him that his ideas were 'more fundamental and inclusive than those of Taylor' and his 'contributions substantially advance the development of unified control systems, which make possible the efficient flow of information about operations that enable managers to control their organizations'.[52]

In addition to these indirect inputs, a more direct approach was followed by a consultant in the 1920s, Wallace Attwood. Attwood was a pioneering consultant in the area of sales and marketing. As an aside to his consultant work, he was a regular contributor to articles in *Sales Management*, a periodical produced by the Cassier Company. As an additional service, together with other 'experts', Attwood formed an advisory panel within this magazine for the provision of advice, free of charge, on a whole range of topics related to selling. Some of these topics were within the field of sales management, with management being a subject at that time that was largely taboo because of the concept that 'managers are born, not made'.[53] He was also by that time becoming well known for his correspondence courses in salesmanship.

As we can see from these few examples of early consultancy in Britain, there is some indication that the concept of education and training was beginning to become an important aspect of consultant services.

This level of importance was raised by the work of Edward Tregaskiss Elbourne, whose entry into the field of consultancy in 1919 also marked his public efforts towards the professionalisation and education for management.[54] Elbourne's contribution effectively commenced with the publication of his book *Factory Administration and Accounts* in 1914 and his energetic programme of lectures to the various professional bodies operating at that time.[55] Elbourne's book raised the notion that management was a subject that could and should be studied.[56] To reflect his status in the profession, following the formation of the Institute of Industrial Administration in 1919, a professional body that Elbourne helped to create, he became the first Honorary Secretary and Honorary Director of Education of the Institute.

Apart from Elbourne's contribution to the process of management education within the Institute and the subsequent adoption of management modules within the syllabuses of some other professional bodies, he was partly responsible for influencing the programme on management held at the Regent Street Polytechnic in London.[57] This programme consisted of a series of twenty-five weekly evening lectures under the broad title of 'Industrial Administration, with Workshop Organisation and Management'.[58]

From October 1923 to March 1924, Elbourne, in co-operation with the Industrial League and Council, organised a series of lectures for students on 'Management and Industry', engaging prominent businessmen as speakers. As a consequence of the lectures and their apparent popularity, the Director of Education of the Regent Street Polytechnic, Major Worswick, created a Department of Industrial Administration at the college. A course on Industrial Administration followed in the September of 1925, covering the subjects of works organisation and management, economics, industrial history, and business practice and statistics. The course was a success and was enlarged in the following year. In 1927, Elbourne became the Joint Director of Studies for the Department of Administration at the Polytechnic. In 1928, Elbourne convinced Worswick that the Polytechnic was the ideal venue for the furtherance of his aim to achieve a professional qualification in industrial administration. Worswick concurred with Elbourne's views and the then two-year course was expanded to a full four years, utilising a syllabus developed by Elbourne himself. The course, taken in three stages, was launched on 24 September 1928, with successful completion of stage three of the course qualifying the individual for an award of a diploma of the Institute. In effect, as far as Britain was concerned, this was the first professional qualification in management. Undoubtedly, in relation to Handy's models (the Professional and Academic approaches), the work of Elbourne as a pioneer provided an important contribution to raising the profile of management within various professional bodies and colleges of further education. There are other examples of individuals – for example, Lyndall Fownes Urwick, Harold Whitehead and T. G. Rose – within consultancy that were prominent in advancing the education of managers during that pre-war period and beyond.[59] However, it is the arrival of the first organised consultancy practice in 1926 (Charles E. Bedaux and Company) that witnessed the true beginnings of the direct role of consultants in management education and training.

The formation of Bedaux company in Britain in 1926 raised the level of training to a formal level as an important element in the delivery of consultancy services. Two specific features of the Bedaux service encouraged the learning process during the course of assignments. Firstly, operatives were trained in the new techniques associated with the processes and working methodologies developed during assignments.[60] In addition, supervisors and operational managers were similarly trained – but fundamental in this approach was the delivery of appreciation courses to senior management, at boardroom level, to ensure 'buy-in' of the new working methods. Secondly, also as part of the service, specially selected personnel, commonly referred to as 'Bedaux Representatives', were trained to ensure continuance of the application at the conclusion of the assignment.[61] These individuals became the forerunners of the management services and training departments of some of Britain's major companies.[62] A good example of this was the work carried out by Bedaux consultants at Imperial Chemical Industries from 1929 in the area of work-study and the creation of training departments in its aftermath.[63] The debate as to whether shop floor changes affected management thinking and practice should consider the scenario of changes that occur when improvements on the shop floor, e.g. raised productivity, and accurate management and financial information, help drive the decision-making process. Consultancy companies formed in the aftermath of Bedaux followed similar examples, although through the process of time the range of services widened and so did the scope of training during assignments. The one exception to this general rule was Harold Whitehead and Staff which, in 1933, was invited by Pitman's Department of Business Development to prepare a correspondence course on salesmanship. At the same time, Whitehead was asked to write a major textbook for wider circulation, entitled 'The Administration of Marketing and Selling'.[64] Both services were provided – correspondence courses became a principal training methodology and form of service provision by the Whitehead company to well into the 1960s and beyond. However, a large portion of work in the field of management education and training, apart from the direct input of training as a consequence of consultancy assignments, remained as a result of lectures and papers to professional bodies.[65] In addition, a whole plethora of textbooks and other publications written by consultants became a major hallmark of their professional approach towards management education and training. That is until the Second World War and post-Second World War periods when more formal and direct methods became of greater significance.

Dealing firstly with the war years, by the commencement of hostilities one or two major companies in Britain had developed in-house training schools to cope with their training needs.[66] This form of training largely dealt with the operational requirements of the firm and had little to do with management per se. In parallel with this, primarily as a consequence of the changing labour base within British industry, there was a requirement for operator training across a range of industries – the active, fit and available young men were conscripted, and women and other males that fell outside of the conscription model took their places in the industrial workforce. This situation was further exacerbated by increases in production of war-supply goods in support of the war effort. Brownlow's chapter, 'Ploughshares into Swords and Back Again', contained a descriptive account of the Second World War period, highlighting the work of consultants primarily at the beginning and the end of the War.[67] Brownlow's generalist approach to the description of events surrounding the activities of management consultants during this period describes a situation in which firms of all types called upon the services of management consultants to change over their production output from peacetime operations to war supply goods.[68] By this, she meant that the demand for consultancy services in the areas of production for 'luxury goods' either fell away or the assignments were terminated. Luxury goods, in large part, were those that held no relevance to war supply production. In addition, many manufacturers changed direction in terms of production output, in some cases quite dramatically, to assist in the war effort. At the end of the war the process was reversed and manufacturers tended to revert to a peacetime production scenario. However, whilst all this was true, the process was more complex. Barnett's exposition of the state of the economy during the Second World War portrays an industrial base lacking the dynamism necessary for sustaining effective output in the face of adversity.[69] His descriptive account of some of the major industries indicates out-of-date production methods, ageing equipment and plant, and a failure to compete on a wide frontage with major competitors elsewhere in the world. This, together with the attitude of the working population in some plants, goes a long way towards explaining why productivity levels were extremely low when compared with countries like Germany and the United States. To a certain extent this was reflected in some of the other factors of production, in this instance the requirement for effective and directed training.

Whilst each of the consultant companies during that period directed effort towards the training of operatives and their supervisors in this changing environment, that effort is exemplified by the work of consultants from Personnel Administration.[70] The company was formed in 1943 by a disillusioned ex-Bedaux engineer (and director), Ernest Edward Butten.[71] Butten had a vision, reflected in the Charter of the company:

> To build PA into the leading organisation of its kind in the world, consisting of men who are acknowledged authorities on the various branches of Management, to create new and improved procedures which can be taught readily to Industrial and Commercial Staffs, and thus raise the standard of Management in the interests of the community as a whole.[72]

Dr A. H. Seymour, who had also previously been a consultant in Bedaux service, joined Butten in this venture. Seymour had, in the years preceding the formation of Personnel Administration, been developing a form of training for operatives that broke tradition with the usual on-site training that had been the common methodology up to that point in time.

This training was called 'Process Analysis Method of Training', but became commonly referred to as the PA Method of Training or PAMT. In short, he developed this training regime 'by combining principles of industrial psychology and work study'. This to be achieved through 'the idea of training to work measurement standards by breaking tasks down into elements and teaching each in detail from the analysis, in psycho-physiological terms, of how the experienced operator performed them'.[73] The training regime was innovatory because it was developed through the application of three separate, but inextricably linked stages:

1 Aptitude tests to determine the suitability of the operator for training in the specific tasks.
2 Training in devices such as light equipment for co-ordinating hand and eye movement.
3 Training for the job, in stages, building up to Experienced Worker Speed (EWS).

The PA Method of Training proved a success and was utilised by many firms during the wartime years and in the post-war period, although various changes in name may have hidden its true origins. At the conclusion of hostilities the system was used for the resettlement of personnel from the three armed services. The name that has survived is 'Skills Analysis Training'. There were a number of advantages to the system when compared with training on-the-job:

1   There was a reduction of scrap and waste as the operator was trained in its avoidance.
2   There were improved relationships on the shop floor as the trained operator was integrated once EWS had been achieved in training. This reduced the likelihood that the output of the department would be brought down by the low output levels associated with on-the-job training.
3   The system provided facilities for existing workers to be re-trained in new skills.
4   There was an overall reduction in training time when compared with on-the-job training. This was reported by the company at being in the region of 50 per cent.

In terms of disadvantages, its major drawback was costs, as trainee operators added little economic value during training. However, probably the most important innovation during the wartime period, and one that fits more closely with the objective of management training, was the opening of the Bedford Work Study School. William Lodge, an ex-Bedaux consultant in the employment of Urwick, Orr and Partners, conceived the School.[74] The School was formed in 1941 with the intention of providing work-study training for consultants' off the job. Initially, the course was of three-week duration in the basic techniques of work-study. The course at Bedford was eventually extended to cover an eight-week programme. By the time it closed its doors in 1961, it had trained 650 students from industry in addition to the volume of training provided to consultants. The real importance of the school was that it partly provided the inspiration for the introduction of management training schools run by the consultant companies in the period after the war. Therefore, from small beginnings the consultant companies launched their management training schools in the years following on from the Second World War. But, before examining the work of these training schools, one event occurred in the aftermath of war that set the scene for management training into the future. That event was the publication in 1947 of the Ministry of Education-commissioned

Urwick Report. Urwick, at the time, was the Chairman of Urwick, Orr and Partners Ltd and a leading member of the 'Management Movement'. The implementation of recommendations from within the report led to the creation of the Certificate and Diploma in Management Studies. However, 'by the 1960s it had awarded only 810 certificates and 640 diplomas, but the revised Diploma in Management Studies (1961) attracted a greater interest'.[75] Urwick had raised the profile of management education and training, at a time when little interest in the subject could be found within business and academic communities alike. Furthermore, there still remained at that time many in business that still believed that 'managers are born, not made'.[76] In the postwar period, the situation changed with regard to the consultant input with the formation of training schools by the larger consultancies for consultants and clients alike.

The management consultant companies had long harboured ideas for the creation of training centres to provide a supporting platform to their work in the operational fields. This was in a similar vein to that of improvements to management practice being also a motivating force in the development of some of the consultant services.[77] Mosson provided a description of the form of training carried out within these schools:

> What many of these institutes have in common is the country house atmosphere, the idea of a withdrawal from active participation in the affairs of industry and commerce to discuss management matters with other managers, to exchange experience and compare notes.[78]

However, the emergence of these schools occurred at a time when the consultant companies themselves had identified the importance of training away from the workplace.[79] Associated Industrial Consultants (AIC), the old Bedaux company, formed a 'College of Management' in 1953 at Dunford College in Sussex. Later, in 1957, AIC provided training services at Bush House, moving subsequently to larger premises at Bilton House in Ealing. This became known as the AIC Staff College. Bilton House was a non-residential centre and, partly as a consequence, training was also conducted on a dispersed basis at other venues. These included, for example, Manchester, Glasgow, Portsmouth and Midhurst. The staff of the 'College' was made up of experienced consultants of the company who, according to Brownlow, had received special training and had an aptitude for teaching.[80] Supplementing the permanent staff, lectures were provided by practising consultants, operational managers and trade union representatives. In addition, some clients of the company provided historical sketches of the work carried out by AIC. To assist with the delivery of lectures, various teaching platforms were applied: the use of films, models, case histories of actual assignments, management games, seminars and syndicate work. Training was thus provided in the following forms:

Site Training: Bespoke training conducted on the client's premises by AIC staff for specially selected personnel (for example foremen and/or charge hands). Training would normally include course work, seminars and/or lectures.

General Training: Usually, non-residential modular training for one or more client staff on an existing AIC staff training course or postgraduate course. Or a bespoke client training package delivered non-residentially at the AIC Staff College.

Central Training: Residential courses provided by AIC at either the Staff College or other suitable venues. Courses usually lasted for between two and three weeks and included guest speakers and evening discussion sessions.[81]

Production Engineering (P-E), the next in terms of longevity, during the war years conducted off-job training for two or three major industrial clients. Consequently, as a logical extension of this experience, in 1953 facilities were developed at Park House at Egham in Surrey for both P-E consultants and client personnel. In parallel to this, training was also delivered at the London Headquarters of the company at Grosvenor Place. Formal training courses were established making use of the previous experience of consultants in the field. Such training was developed utilising, what was considered by the company to be, up-to-date thinking in both functional and management subjects.[82] Urwick, Orr and Partners Ltd, utilising their experiences at the Bedford Work-Study School and the personal ambitions of its founder, formed a management training centre at Slough in 1947 for the provision of training to client staff.[83] The Slough Training Centre was the first external management training school set up by a consultant company in this country specifically to deliver training in general management subjects, and both centres (Slough and Bedford) operated in parallel in the ensuing years. Initially, at Slough there was just one course of eight weeks in general management. Within a short time, however, a number of specialist options were included that broadened the scope of the training. These options were production, marketing (known at that time as distribution) and finance (known at that time as control).

The major contribution to management training, however, came through the setting up of the Urwick Management Centre that was established at Baylis House following a conversion programme. This occurred primarily because the Slough Training Centre became too small to support the demand for providing training services. Its inadequacy stemmed from the fact that it was a listed building and, consequently, the company was unable to expand the premises. Similarly, in 1953 Personnel Administration obtained a building suitable for the establishment of a management training centre. Sundridge Park, at Bromley in Kent, opened its doors in 1953 for the purpose of training managers in short courses appropriate to their roles. As a testimonial to the demand for the delivery of training at Sundridge Park, this remains the only management training centre of the original four providing training services to the present day.

Inevitably, it is possible to argue that what was on offer was not an education but a regime in which the exchange of information was facilitated to provide advancement in management knowledge. In other words, the consultants had facilitated the process of management development at a more formal level. These were consultants who only a few years earlier had largely concentrated their efforts in the direction of operational efficiency within the work place. At the same time, until the formation of the Work-Study School at Bedford, training in the basic techniques of work-study and labour cost control was conducted on the job for consultants. The subsequent knowledge of these techniques was passed on to client personnel for further advancement within the firm during the course of assignments, and not as a separate formal course of instruction. Therefore, the creation of management training centres was a major step forward at time when little else was occurring in the furtherance of management education and training within Britain. The effort of consultant companies in the field of management training was confirmed during a conference arranged by the Federation of British Industries (FBI) on 27 April 1961.

At this conference, representatives of British universities, colleges of further education, the Henley Management Centre, government departments, interested parties from business and the consultant community reviewed and debated the situation with a view to taking forward the issue of management education and training. Certainly, the evidence provided by the universities and further education colleges confirmed the situation described by Handy and other commentators referenced in this article in that an ad hoc array of courses with no defined progressive path was the general situation that still existed at the beginning of the 1960s. However, the conference, aptly named 'Stocktaking on

Management Education', did enable precisely that to occur. Lyndall Fownes Urwick represented the management consultants and provided a background paper.[84] This detailed the services provided in this field by the then members of the Management Consultancies Association (MCA).[85] As a consequence of this article, it is possible to identify the services provided by consultants within six principal areas:

1   The number of student weeks of management training provided.
2   Student throughput.
3   The number of firms assisted in forming their own management training facilities.
4   The number of external lectures delivered.
5   The number of books and booklets produced.
6   The number of articles published.

These are summarised in Table 1.1 for the period between 1940 and 1960.
In terms of the direct role of consultants, 'Student Weeks of Management Training', 'Student Throughput' and 'Firms Assisted in Starting Their Own Management Training Regimes' are the categories

Table 1.1 Direct and Indirect Educational Inputs

Educational Input[86]	Prior to 1956	1956	1957	1958	1959	1960	Total
Direct Inputs							
Student Weeks of Management Training	11,858	6,725	8,220	8,672	9,217	10,360	55,052
Student Throughput	2,276	942	1,401	1,603	1,549	1,547	9,318
Firms Assisted in Starting Their Own Management Training Regimes	99	33	34	44	50	50	310
Educational Input	*Prior to 1956*	*1956*	*1957*	*1958*	*1959*	*1960*	*Total*
Indirect Inputs							
Summary of Lectures Delivered	1,815	470	367	359	332	443	3,786
Summary of Books and Booklets Produced	64	15	17	17	15	17	145
Summary of Articles Published	257	63	81	83	70	81	635

Source: L. F. Urwick, 'The Part Played By the Management Consultant'.

associated with this field. With the exception of assistance provided to firms, most of the direct inputs were made possible through the formation of the consultant company training schools by the member companies of the MCA in the post-war period. These inputs could be categorised as falling within two broad headings:

Functional methods and techniques, for example work-study, organisation and methods (O&M), production control and method-study.
Specialist subjects, for example general management, finance, marketing and operational research.

In terms of duration, these courses lasted from a matter of days through to a number of months, with the orientation towards specialist subjects becoming more prevalent through the course of time. However, it is through an analysis of this data that it is possible to develop the concept of trends.

An important factor to emerge from Table 1.1 is the take-up rate for training courses ('Student Throughput'). This initially increased during the period (1956–1960) and then levelled off for the remainder of the decade. The principal reason for this was that as some courses were changed, or were replaced by others, in some of the centres, their durations tended to lengthen as either more detail was added or additional modules were included. In addition, there was a growing emphasis on specialist management subjects. These tended to be of longer duration than the functional method and technique-orientated courses. However, until full capacity was reached, there was an overall growth of 54 per cent in the number of 'Student Weeks of Management Training' for the period between 1956 and 1960. While the average indicated an annual growth rate of approximately 11 per cent per year, this may be somewhat misleading as trends within individual companies fluctuated on a yearly basis, even though generally growth was the dominant feature for each of the member companies of the MCA. In terms of the other form of direct inputs featured in this article, 'Firms Assisted in Starting Their Own Management Training Regimes', there was a growing trend in the period 1956–1960. In percentage terms, there was a rise in demand of 51 per cent over the five years, or in real terms a 10 per cent rise on a yearly basis. Although there were similar fluctuations between companies to that of 'Student Throughput', overall, the increased delivery of training to staff of client companies and to other managers provides an indication of a growing demand for formalised training. When compared with all else that was going on in the wider world of education and training for management within Britain, the consultants' contribution was clearly important, at least during the period of the 1950s, and previously. However, turning to the indirect inputs, these appeared less progressive. In fact, to some large measure, the data indicate a trend in which at the mid-point within Table 1.1 there was a fall in the level of output. There is no real reason why this should have occurred, other than possibly the increased demand for consultant services generally during this period would have prevented time being spent on these indirect outputs.

A review of the situation in the 1960s and 1970s with regard to the member companies of the MCA indicates that the importance of direct training inputs in terms of courses provided to client staff and other customers was a significant feature of consultant practice. For example, in 1963 there were 265 training courses run by the member companies of the Association.[87] By 1972, ten years later, this figure had increased to 882, a growth rate of over 300 per cent. This mirrored the growth rate in consultancy generally. However, from the mid-1970s, even though the number of member firms of the MCA increased the total number of courses began to fall. This may be partly explained by the increase in training providers generally within Britain. The consultants had played a significant role, but attitudes were changing. This is reflected in the range of educational and training providers, not the least of which were the universities, which were becoming increasingly important as management education providers. Therefore, while the heyday of the consultants was over, they had provided in some large measure the impetus for change. Their growing numbers, the types of services provided and their training inputs were all important features.[88] This peculiar combination of training methods was reflected in their model of training delivery, 'The Consultancy Approach'.

IV. The Consultancy Approach – a summarisation and conclusion

The previous section identified the work of management consultants in the general areas of management education and training through two distinct roles, direct and indirect. This final section of the article brings together the various threads and compares it with Handy's three approaches described within the second section.[89] This comparison will indicate that not only was the Consultant Approach distinctive in its own right and, therefore, should be treated as a separate model, but that many of the elements of the Consultancy Approach could found within Handy's existing three models.

Handy largely excluded the input of consultants, including their coaching during assignments, although he recognised that they had played a form of direct role within the Corporate Approach. This recognition ignored the fact that historically consultants were intimately engaged in activities in support of all three models developed within his thesis. The previous section highlights much of that involvement. At the same time, the work of consultants in the broad fields of management education and training does not comfortably reside solely within any of the Approaches described by Handy. It is this contention and the importance of the work of consultants, in their own right, that mark out their contributions as unique and, therefore, justifiably they should be recognised for their own distinctive approach. Taking each of Handy's models in turn, this summarisation will indicate the distinctive nature of the Consultancy Approach.

Dealing first with the Academic Approach, this is a description of the part played by universities, polytechnics and colleges of further education. During the period covered by this article (1869 to the mid-1980s), public institutions tended to be largely inactive in terms of their contribution to the development of management, although within the private sector there are indications of growth. That is with the exception of those colleges involved with delivering courses in support of the attainment of qualifications for a number of professional institutes. Nevertheless, from the 1950s onwards this trend within the universities and colleges of further education began to change (these changes have been highlighted in section one). This is further emphasised through the formation of two university business schools in the mid-1960s and, thereafter, through an expanding range of courses in an increasing number of institutions. Prior to the 1960s, courses delivered by universities in part only lay on the fringes of management, but without a specific managerial orientation. The colleges of further education played their part, in the main, with regard to the functional aspects of management until the arrival of the Certificate and Diploma in Management Studies, but then on a limited scale until changes occurred in the course content in the 1960s. However, until more recently, their orientation was largely vocational and this form of approach, in any event, fitted more closely with Handy's Professional model. The relationship of consultants with the academic community stretched back almost as far as the birth of consultancy itself. If we ignore any indirect contributions in terms of the delivery of lectures at academic venues or the publications which highlighted that management as a subject could be taught, we cannot ignore the contributions made by individuals such as Elbourne and others in the pursuance of academic excellence for the subject of management within some colleges in terms of both professional qualifications and the functional aspects of management. For example, the report commissioned by the Ministry of Education in the immediate post-war period, commonly known as the 'Urwick Report'. This led to the Certificate and Diploma in Management Studies. Another example is the contribution made by consultants to the debate relating to the future of management education and training. In that debate, parties from all areas that had an interest in education and training came together in an attempt to highlight the importance of management as a subject for teaching into the future.[90] However, there is another relationship that tends to be ignored, and one that has not been mentioned previously, that of the crossover between academic and consultant, and vice versa. In the early days, this crossover is exemplified by the work of Dr Harold Whitehead, an American academic of British birth who combined consultancy with academia in the United States, and on his return to this country combined consultancy with his leading position in the 'Management Movement'.[91] There are many examples of academics becoming consultants and consultants assuming academic roles throughout the history of the consulting industry. Nowadays, some academic institutions have their own consultancy arms and the link between consultants and academics is an ever strengthening one.[92] All these relationships provide examples of the work of consultants within the broad area described by Handy as the Academic Approach.

There is another relationship that this article has highlighted, that of the relationship between the Academic Approach and the Professional Approach. The Professional Approach is a model described by Handy as a method of training delivery that followed a structured methodology, in that it culminated in a professional qualification, and possibly membership of a particular professional body. Within this particular model, the work of consultants can be identified through both forms of role. From the very beginnings of management consultancy, the delivery of papers and lectures to professional bodies became a hallmark of their service. Some examples have been provided within this article, but a search of the archives of professional associations will indicate the depth of that involvement.[93] This was because management consultancy had its roots within the professions, especially within the engineering and accountancy professions.[94] In addition to this, the development of professional recognition in management and management consultancy was a subject that was important to leading members and firms within the consultancy industry. Once again, the roots of this movement are centred within the early part of the twentieth century, exemplified through the efforts of E. T. Elbourne and the formation of the Institute of Industrial Administration. The relationship between the Academic Approach and the Professional Approach lies within the venues used for the delivery of training leading to those professional qualifications within the field of management, for example the Diploma of the Institute of Industrial Administration awarded through successful study at the Regent Street Polytechnic and elsewhere.[95] The Certificate and Diploma in Management Studies, especially, became a bridging mechanism between academia and the professions, with courses being delivered at various colleges of further education within Britain. The work of consultants within the professions is all too evident, even to the present day, following the formation of their own professional bodies in the 1950s and 1960s, the Management Consultancies Association and the Institute of Management Consultants, respectively. However, as this article has emphasised, it is within the Corporate Approach that Handy pointed to the work of consultants.

The Corporate Approach is largely to do with the delivery of in-house training by some of the major businesses in this country. Examples quoted by Handy include ICI, Shell and Unilever. This style is concerned with the development of role-specific training, culminating in general management training when the individual reaches a more senior position within the firm. The involvement of consultants within this general model centres on their direct role, specifically training delivered as part of an assignment, as well as assistance provided to firms in setting up their own management training centres. One really need go back no earlier than the formation of the Bedaux company in 1926 to identify the involvement of consultants in both these aspects of the Corporate Approach. However, it is the work of consultants identified within Table 1.1 for the period leading up to the 1960s that highlights their involvement within this particular method. Therefore, overall, the work of management consultants supports the contention that it spanned all three Approaches developed by Handy. In addition, Handy's failure to fit the Consultant Approach into any of his other models is clearly misleading, especially given the aspects of education and training that fall outside of these models for which the consultants can be identified as playing a key role.

Examples of such methods include the development of operator training, both on and off-site, the development of correspondence courses and involvement in the Training Within Industry scheme. Two other notable examples are those associated with management training delivered with the consultancy companies' management training schools and the writing of books that were developed as practical guides for managers in the pursuit of excellence and effectiveness within the workplace. These aspects were particularly important at a time when both the business and academic communities were doing very little to support the requirements for management education and training. This was especially at a time when it was still perceived in many quarters that 'managers are born, not made', a point supported by Shanks in his review of the management consulting industry in the mid-1960s.[96] Therefore, the Consultancy Approach, as a model for education and training delivery, is the combination of the direct and indirect aspects of consultants' service deployment described in the previous sections. In addition, the model as a whole is strongly linked to those other models developed by Handy.

Therefore, there are two aspects to the Consultancy Approach; the unique package of training delivery provided by consultants progressively throughout their history, and the part played by the consultant within the other three models developed by Handy. These contributions are important and should not be ignored because they were occurring at a time when little else was going on, especially in the period prior to the mid-1960s. The management consultants, in their heyday, were in the vanguard of management education and training, losing ground only when attitudes began to change towards the role of education in management. That change brought with it an increasing number of training establishments and public sector providers delivering courses in the fields of management and business.

Notes

* This article is largely based on Chapter 6 of M. Ferguson, *The Origin, Gestation and Evolution of Management Consultancy within Britain (1869–1965): The Principles, Practices and Techniques of a New Professional Grouping* (unpublished PhD thesis, Open University, 1999).

1 L. F. Urwick (the then Chairman of Urwick, Orr and Partners Ltd), 'The Part Played by the Management Consultant', in *Stocktaking on Management Education* (Federation of British Industries, conference papers, 27 April 1961).

2 National Economic Development Office, *The Making of Managers* (HMSO, 1967).

3 C. Handy, C. Gordon, I. Gow and C. Randlesome (hereinafter known as Handy et al.), *Making Managers* (London: Pitman Publishing, 1988).

4 Handy et al., *Making Managers*, pp. 163–191.

5 For a full account of the history of management consulting in Britain to the period of the mid-1960s see Ferguson, *The Origin, Gestation and Evolution of Management Consultancy within Britain*.

6 S. P. Keeble, *The Ability to Manage: A Study of British Management, 1890–1990* (Manchester: Manchester University Press, 1992), pp. 52–54.

7 This situation is confirmed by Handy in the next section where his models of management education and training point towards three different 'Approaches', each of which contains choices that do not appear to support a progressive career path for the individual.

8 Keeble, *The Ability to Manage*, pp. 52–54.

9 G. Millerson, *The Qualifying Associations: A Study in Professionalization* (London: Routledge and Kegan Paul, 1964) quoted in Keeble, *The Ability to Manage*, pp. 52–54.

10 That majority came, inevitably, with the appearance of a large group of new Labour Members of Parliament that had not previously served in the House of Commons.

11 These experiences were exemplified by the high levels of unemployment throughout the period between the two World Wars.

12 All initiatives had been determined prior to the General Election.

13 P. King-Scott, *The Institution of Industrial Managers: A History* (London: The Institution of Industrial Managers, 1991), p. 12.

14 A. Silberston, *Education and Training for Industrial Management: A Critical Survey* (London: Management Publications Ltd, 1955), pp. 25–55. This book was based on an analysis conducted by the author during the period 1950–1954 in which he examined the contributions of various training institutions within Britain. The institutions included were technical colleges, universities, residential commercial providers, internal company training programmes and other miscellaneous providers, including the Training Within Industry scheme.

15 Whilst the Certificate and Diploma in Management was viewed as a step forward, only 810 certificates and 640 diplomas had been awarded by the beginning of the 1960s (Keeble, *The Ability to Manage*, p. 151). In 1961 a revised Diploma in Management Studies, with the Certificate no longer offered as a formal qualification or course, witnessed a greater take up than its predecessor. However, it still remained a course taken by an individual during his/her working lifetime and not as a pre-experience event.

16 J. F. Wilson, *British Business History, 1720–1994* (Manchester: Manchester University Press, 1995), pp. 161–163; Federation of British Industries, *Stocktaking on Management Education.*

17 J. F. Wilson, *The Manchester Experiment: A History of Manchester Business School 1965–1990* (London: Paul Chapman Publishing Ltd, 1992), p. 7.

18 John Bolton and Keith Joseph were the founders, and the Foundation was an important force in the 1960s and beyond with regard to education for management in the universities.

19 This was despite the efforts of the Foundation for Management Education, in the early –1960s, and the formation of two business schools at Manchester and London in the mid-1960s.

20 The 'Conspectus' series of booklets covered seven editions from 1953 through to 1968. The first three editions were titled *Education and Training in the Field of Management* (1953; 1954/1955; 1956), with the final four editions titled *A Conspectus of Management Courses* (1960; 1963; 1965; 1968). The booklets contained information supplied to the British Institute of Management by the training providers themselves and there was

no attempt by the Institute to provide a judgement on the quality of education and training delivery. However, whilst the content and format of each edition varied, education and training providers fell within three broad groups: universities, colleges and independent centres. These covered between them courses within the areas of general management, functional management, management techniques, management skills, background subjects and the qualifications of the professional institutes.

21 British Institute of Management, *Education and Training in the Field of Management* (London: British Institute of Management, 1953).

22 Silberston, *Education and Training for Industrial Management*, pp. 25–55.

23 British Institute of Management, *A Conspectus of Management Courses: Education and Training in the Field of Management* (London: British Institute of Management, 1963).

24 British Institute of Management, *Education and Training in the Field of Management* (London: British Institute of Management, Vol. I, 1955).

25 British Institute of Management, *A Conspectus of Management Courses* (London: British Institute of Management, 1968). At twenty universities within the 'Universities – Reference Grid' of this publication departments indicated such titles.

26 First appearing in the British Institute of Management, *A Conspectus of Management Courses: Education and Training in the Field of Management* (London: British Institute of Management, 1963).

27 British Institute of Management, *A Conspectus of Management Courses* (London: British Institute of Management, 1968).

28 From the sixteen private institutions featured within British Institute of Management, *Education and Training in the Field of Management* (London: British Institute of Management, Vol. II, 1955) the numbers rose to forty-three in British Institute of Management, *A Conspectus of Management Courses* (London: British Institute of Management, 1968).

29 Wilson, *The Manchester Experiment*, p. 50.

30 National Economic Development Office, *The Making of Managers*; Handy et al., *Making Managers*.

31 This distinction is necessary because British consultants have played a role in the education and development of managers in numerous countries as a consequence of their international operations.

32 Handy et al., *Making Managers*, p. 163.

33 Handy et al., *Making Managers*, p. 168.

34 Handy et al., *Making Managers*, p. 166.

35 Handy et al., *Making Managers*, p. 170.

36 Handy et al., *Making Managers*, p. 173.

37 Handy et al., *Making Managers*, p. 169. This is the only indication provided in Handy's three Approaches of the work of management consultants and, then, only within the context of a supporting agent within the Corporate model. Presumably, the recognition of the work of consultants related largely to the training consultancies or consultancies that provided training as a prominent service within their portfolios. This is because this had become a growing feature of the consultancy industry by the period of the 1980s and beyond, remaining a phenomenon up until the present day. However, training was and is an aspect of traditional consultancy services, and this is covered in more detail in the final two sections of this article.

38 Handy et al., *Making Managers*, p. 170.
39 Handy et al., *Making Managers*, p. 173.
40 Urwick, *The Part Played by the Management Consultant.*
41 Ferguson, *The Origin, Gestation and Evolution of Management Consultancy within Britain.* The first identified instance of the work of management consultants occurred as a result of a series of advertisements placed in *The Engineer* in 1869 by Montague Whitmore, simply entitled 'Avoid Losses and Failures'.
42 There are no recorded instances of women involved in management consulting in Britain until the period of the late 1930s/early 1940s. The early consultants were all male, and they either had a background in engineering or accountancy, although there were a few in marketing, tending to operate in the engineering and manufacturing sectors.
43 The company confusingly changed its name a number of times during its lifetime: Charles E. Bedaux Ltd; British Bedaux Ltd; Associated Industrial Consultants (AIC) and INBUCON (Industrial and Business Consultants).
44 The company was renamed in the 1940s to Harold Whitehead and Partners and survives to the present day on a small scale.
45 In the mid-1930s, the company further widened its portfolio of services to include production efficiency.
46 This was because the founder, Ernest Butten, was an ex-Bedaux consultant and director who was tied to a severance agreement that stated that he would not practice as a consultant or run a competing consultant company for a period of two years. The precise nature of the restriction related to the provision of services in work-study and labour cost control, the main areas of consultancy at that time.
47 The Whitehead company did not grow and expand at the rate of the other companies, and never grew larger than an all-up total (support and consulting) of one hundred staff. However, this should not detract from its importance as a specialised service provider and pioneering consultant organisation.
48 The term the 'Big Four' was generally applied to these four companies (P. Tisdall, *Agents of Change: The Development and Practice of Management Consultancy* (London: William Heinemann Ltd, 1982), p. 59). That is until their relative position within the market was challenged by the growing number of consultants employed within the consultancy arms of some of the major accountancy practices in the mid- to late 1960s (Ferguson, *The Origin, Gestation and Evolution of Management Consultancy within Britain*, pp. 371–375). However, their share of the market is reflected in the number of consultants operating in Britain during this period and general estimates of this indicate approximately 75 per cent (L. Tatham, *The Efficiency Experts: An Impartial Survey of Management Consultancy* (London: Business Publications Ltd, 1964), pp. 51–52; Ferguson, *The Origin, Gestation and Evolution of Management Consultancy within Britain*, p. 398).
49 Norcross was later taken over by A. T. Kearney in 1969 as a means of establishing its position within Britain.
50 The first recorded instance of an activity that fits within the definition of management consulting occurred in the period 1869–1870. Very few historical records of the activities of early consultant pioneers survive to the

present day but attention was drawn to Whitmore through an advertisement that he placed in *The Engineer* during 1869 which was simply entitled 'Avoid Losses and Failures'. This was a reference to a cost management system for installation into factories and engineering workshops. However, costing should not be confused with accountancy; cost accounting as an activity, and as a mode of service delivery, has a relationship with traditional accounting methods only from the perspective that it uses financial information from the business. Traditional methods of accounting enable accountants to 'allocate costs on the basis of past operations, but not know how to use these costs to predict the future' (M. Chatfield, *A History of Accounting Thought* (New York: Robert E. Krieger Publishing Company, 1977), pp. 104–105). Costing, or more precisely cost recording, review and control, enabled an assessment of both the present and a prediction of the future. This provided information that was fundamental to the efficient operation of the business. Equally, costing was related to the operational aspects of production. In this way, it provided timely information on the effective deployment and usage of all the various forms of resources, including labour. All of this was in addition to providing financial information to assist in pricing and profit allocation calculations.

51 However, there were probably no more than about twenty individuals performing the role of management consultants at any one time during the period of 1869–1926. The majority of work was carried out in the engineering and manufacturing sectors, and the forms of services provided lay in the direction of costing and production planning and control.

52 M. Jelinek, 'Towards systematic management: Alexander Hamilton Church', *Business History Review*, Spring 1980, p. 71.

53 Wilson, *British Business History*, pp. 161–163.

54 Elbourne formed a consulting partnership with Sir Harry Brindley, Messrs Brindley and Elbourne, Consulting Engineers of 110 Victoria Street, London, SW 1. This was the first recorded instance of the usage of the term 'consulting' within the title of a management consulting organisation in this country.

55 E. T. Elbourne, *Factory Administration and Accounts* (London: Longmans & Co., 1914). The book sold 10,000 copies during the period of the Fist World War, largely as a consequence of individuals within the Ministry of Munitions who viewed it as essential to standardising the operations of an array of contracting firms that supplied the Ministry at that time. Elbourne's book had, in effect, raised the profile of the notion that management was a subject that could be studied. This was a movement away from the traditional idea that the manager's job was made up of a series of ill-defined responsibilities and functions, in other words one that could not be taught.

56 T. G. Rose, *A History of the Institute of Industrial Administration, 1919–1951* (London: Pitman, 1954).

57 Two professional bodies that included management modules within their syllabi were the Institute of Mechanical Engineers and the Institute of Electrical Engineers. The course at the Regent Street Polytechnic began in 1923, with the Polytechnic becoming the Polytechnic of Central London in the 1960s, and, following the reorganisation of polytechnics in the 1990s, was renamed the University of Westminster.

58 E. F. L. Brech, *Productivity in Perspective* (Milton Keynes: The Open University, 1991), pp. 47–48.

59 These individuals were also prominent within the 'Management Movement' at that time.

60 The main thrust of Bedaux services at that time lay in the direction of productivity improvements and wage payment mechanisms within manufacturing enterprises.

61 For a full account of the history of the Bedaux company, see M. Brownlow, *The History of Inbucon* (unpublished company history, 1972).

62 Ferguson, *The Origin, Gestation and Evolution of Management Consultancy within Britain*, pp. 409–410.

63 J. E. Faraday, *The Story of Work Study in Imperial Chemical Industries* (internal ICI historical account of the spread of work-study and training, 1961); M. Ferguson, *Charles Eugene Bedaux 1886–1955: The Man Whom Time Forgot* (Open University occasional paper, December 1996).

64 H. Whitehead, *The Administration of Marketing and Selling* (London: Sir Isaac Pitman & Sons, 1937).

65 For example, see the input of Lyndall Fownes Urwick in this indirect approach to management education and training in Urwick, Orr and Partners Ltd, *L. Urwick: A Bibliography* (London: The Sheneval Press Ltd, 1958).

66 For example ICI, see Faraday, *The Story of Work Study*.

67 Brownlow, *A History of Inbucon*, pp. 51–66.

68 Brownlow, *A History of Inbucon*, pp. 53–54.

69 C. Barnett, *The Audit of War: The Illusion and Reality of Britain as a Great Nation* (London: Pan, 1996).

70 This is supervision and management at all levels within the firm.

71 His frustrations with the company were largely to do with his perception of its lack of energy in terms of expansion and lack of vision in terms of resourcing.

72 A. Fogg, *PA's Early History* (PA Consulting Group historical document, 1980), p. 6. The aspirations detailed within the 'Charter' were limited in the first two years of the company's existence owing to the constraints placed upon Butten by his previous contract of employment with the Bedaux company. Partly because of this, at least initially, the Personnel Administration developed a service provision base concerned with the application of techniques in the training environment.

73 W. D. Seymour, *Skills Analysis Training: A Handbook for Managers, Supervisors and Instructors* (London: Sir Isaac Pitman & Sons Ltd, 1968).

74 The title 'School' may seem somewhat grandiose in the light of the fact that it was the living room of Lodge's house. But this should not take away its importance as, probably, the first school in Britain concentrating on management techniques for a customer base that included consultants and industrial managers. Lodge was an older man who did not wish to work as a consultant under the pressures of wartime service.

75 Keeble, *The Ability to Manage*, p. 151.

76 Wilson, *British Business History*, pp. 161–163.

77 Ferguson, *The Origin, Gestation and Evolution of Management Consultancy within Britain*, p. 202.

78 T. M. Mosson, *Management Education in Five European Countries* (London: Business Publications Ltd, 1965), p. 191.

79 Prior to the Second World War consultant recruit training was almost exclusively carried out on the job with an experienced consultant. Invariably, the training was structured to the extent that a definitive list of skills

had to be learnt and practised, and the recruit was marked on his progress through tests, but the order and duration varied from recruit to recruit. This was because no two assignments were the same, each had different requirements and some recruits were required to attend and train at more than one assignment. In addition, each experienced consultant developed his or her own styles and standards.

80 Brownlow, *A History of Inbucon*, pp. 82–84.
81 Brownlow, *A History of Inbucon*, pp. 82–84. The training school survived until the demise of the company in the 1980s when it was subsumed into P-E.
82 PE, *Fifty Years of Professional Enterprise: The Story of P-E* (London: S. Straker and Sons Ltd, 1984), pp. 17–18.
83 Urwick made public his ambitions in an address to the Office Managers Association in 1938 when he defined the major contributions which a competent consultant may be expected to make as accurate diagnosis, effective remedies and creative business research. In addition, he stated that an important contribution was that of providing, 'inspiration and training of the clients' staff in a new and better approach to management problems' (G. Sanders, 'The Urwick Management Centre', in *Keeping in Touch*, 60th Anniversary Edition, Journal of the UOP Keeping in Touch Association No. 58, 1994, p. 10).
84 Urwick, *The Part Played By The Management Consultant*.
85 The MCA, formed in 1956, estimated that at that time (1961) the membership of the Association accounted for 80 per cent (1,200 consultants) of the total number of consultants operating in this country. Regardless of whether such an estimation was completely accurate, the member companies were certainly the largest individually by far of those that operated in Britain at that time and, therefore, such an estimation would have been reasonable. The member companies of the MCA at that time were Associated Industrial Consultants (formerly Bedaux), Production Engineering (now part of Lorien Consulting), Urwick, Orr and Partners, Personnel Administration (now PA), Harold Whitehead & Partners, Harold Norcross and Partners, the Anne Shaw Organisation and Industrial Administration.
86 In terms of the total data there were weaknesses in that the data on student weeks and student throughput prior to 1956 was not available for Associated Industrial Consultants or Personnel Administration.
87 Data obtained from the annual reports of the Management Consultancies Association for the period 1960s through to the 1980s.
88 Ferguson, *The Origin, Gestation and Evolution of Management Consultancy within Britain*, p. 235. Growth can be associated with the increase in the number of consultants generally and the switch in emphasis away from production productivity assignments towards those areas in client firms where management was primarily the main concern.
89 Handy et al., *Making Managers*.
90 Federation of British Industries Stocktaking on Management Education.
91 Whitehead was the chairman of Harold Whitehead and Staff featured in this article. He, together with other leading consultants, played a prominent role within the 'Management Movement' in this country. For an account of the work of some of these individuals, see J. Child, *British*

Management Thought (London: George Allen and Unwin Ltd, 1969). However, Whitehead was primarily a consultant who was drawn to academia as a consequence of the work he was carrying out in the United States at that time.

92 For an example of the relationship between academia and consultancy, see F. Davidson, *Management Consultants* (London: Thomas Nelson and Sons Ltd, 1972).

93 For example, a search of the archives of the professional bodies associated with accountancy and engineering will reveal a rich tapestry of materials. The majority of these materials relate to papers delivered at professional venues and articles written for a professional and technical readership.

94 At least to the period of the 1960s, the overwhelming majority of consultants were established professional practitioners, mainly from the engineering and accountancy professions. It was not until the advent of the computer and the creation of business schools that large numbers entered the consultancy industry without such a background. See Ferguson, *The Origin, Gestation and Evolution of Management Consultancy within Britain*, pp. 371–377.

95 Even outside of the management field, links are apparent. For example, in 1925 the Institute of Mechanical Engineers instituted in its examination for professional membership a compulsory module (Section C) 'Economics of Engineering with Workshop Organisation and Management'.

96 J. F. Wilson, *British Business History*, pp. 161–163; M. Shanks, 'Management consultants: Breaking through the British boardroom', *The Director*, May 1964, p. 269.

2 Visible hands and visible handles

Understanding the managerial revolution in the UK

John Quail

Introduction

This study is designed to attempt to find ground rules for understanding the process of the managerial revolution in Britain. Such a study is necessary because firstly it is little understood, secondly it was late – not completed until the 1980s – and third the consequences of this revolution are continuing and profound. These assertions are set out in more explanatory detail below after a study of the various formulations of the concept of the managerial revolution. This study will examine the shortcomings of existing formulations in the face of the actual development of managerialist firms and a managerialist society in Britain. A potentially more powerful conceptual framework derived from the work of Michel Foucault will then be proposed as providing a best fit for developments in the UK.

The managerial revolution

The managerial revolution is a term which is commonly used, but is the subject of a number of definitions and teleologies which are not necessarily consistent and sometimes poorly theorised. All of them have some sense of the 'shock of the new' – hence the use of the word revolution – and all of them share the sense that both organisations and society are changed by the developments they describe. Roughly four meanings of the managerial revolution can be derived from the literature:

1   a world-wide social/political phenomenon as set out in the work of James Burnham[1] and Bruno Rizzi[2]
2   the consequence of the large-scale divorce of ownership and control in joint stock companies in various authors following Berle and Means[3]

DOI: 10.4324/9781003206996-2

3   as the triumph of managerial co-ordination over market co-ordination in the work of A. D. Chandler[4]
4   as competitive advantage in A. D. Chandler,[5] J.-J. Servan-Schreiber[6] and H. Perkin.[7]

We will take these in order.

The works of Burnham – who created the phrase 'the managerial revolution' – and Rizzi are the unorthodox offspring of debates in the pre-Second World War Trotskyist movement on the nature of the Soviet Union. Both writers characterise the USSR, fascist Germany and Italy, European social democracy and the US New Deal as disparate parts of a common process leading to a post-capitalist, post-democratic world of managed societies. These various societies represent the emergence and rise to power of a new managerial class. Burnham also used the work of Berle and Means (see below) to add the organic changes within US capitalism to his general argument. Burnham has been strongly criticised for conceptual confusion and for political predictions which soon foundered.[8] The wider political element of his thinking is of little concern to us in this study but the general stress in his work on the wider interaction between changes in large political and business institutions is very relevant. The idea that the managerial revolution is the product or project of a revolutionary managerial class is one that we will discuss briefly later.

The work of Berle and Means on the 'silent revolution'[9] in American business in the 1930s has been followed by a large number of studies and debates.[10] Their argument was that an increasing number of US corporations had separated ownership and control: share ownership was large and diffuse, the managers of the corporations had minimal ownership stakes and held power by position rather than property right. The separation of ownership and control, as we have seen, is an element in Burnham's arguments; it is an important plank in Chandler's arguments (see below) and for Nichols it is the very 'quintessence of managerialism' in his dated but still useful study.[11] Some authors clearly expected much to flow from the increasing divorce of ownership and control. Even where no great social disruption on the lines proposed by Burnham is expected, a distinct change in social style is predicted by some writers. In a later work, Berle[12] claims that the removal of property interest from corporate control has removed the cause of conflict in industry and society allowing a new era of corporate responsibility and social consensus. Dahrendorf[13] believed that the key relationship in the industrial organisation is authority, whether an organisation is dominated by owners or managers. What changes with the shift between the two is the nature of the legitimacy of the authority. In manager-dominated enterprise some kind of consensus between the manager and the managed is required. Managerialist economists like Marris[14] have argued that with the divorce of ownership and control, satisfactory rather than maximum returns to shareholders is the order of the day.

Events have placed a certain perspective on the debates briefly outlined above. Two decades of neo-liberal economic policy and globalisation have reduced the restraints on companies: corporate responsibility and social consensus are now largely optional matters for most large corporations. The power of financial institutions, particularly in the USA and UK, has grown so that they have great power over the business strategies of many corporations, particularly their dividend policy. Strategies now common in the USA and UK of tying senior management interests to those of shareholders through the use of stock options has blurred the boundary between ownership and control once more. Large corporations no longer hesitate to rationalise their organisations and make employees redundant in a manner which does not indicate a seeking of consensus with those they manage. In its outward manifestations what we have is a capitalism that is vigorous and domineering.

The underlying assumption in Berle, Dahrendorf, Marris and others appears to be – at least in part – that the absence of property interest in those at the top of a corporation implies a lessening of legitimacy, which means in turn that autocracy should be modified by consensus and a becoming social restraint. It is a message that top corporate management appears not to have heeded. It may well be that the significance of the divorce of ownership and control for mid-twentieth-century commentators was that it appeared to undermine the legal basis of joint stock company governance which had been in place for a century: the duty of directors as shareholders themselves to conduct the business in the best interests of the shareholders as whole. From the distance of 2002, the concern that management might not be legitimised by property rights appears to be as relevant to the development of managerialism as the gold standard is to sound national finance. The divorce of ownership and control as traditionally understood now appears to be perhaps no more than a symptom of the growing size of corporations, possibly a necessary but certainly not a sufficient condition for the managerial revolution.

A. D. Chandler's well-known account of the managerial revolution in American business proposes a more nuanced process. *The Visible Hand*[15] is the history of the development of administrative structures of a particular type which allowed unprecedentedly large US corporations to mobilise and maximise their economic power by overcoming the dysfunctionalities of scale. The growth of these companies was the consequence of a large and expanding US market which encouraged mass production and mass distribution. The volume of production and the scale of distribution that ensued required new administrative structures and methods to manage them. These structures and methods reduced the costs of internally managed transactions below the costs of these transactions in the market. The resulting efficiencies allowed these large companies to grow further.

Chandler's work only briefly deals with the wider sociological ramifications of the rise of the large professionally managed corporation. Nevertheless, his incremental version of the rise of US managerial capitalism does conclude that a process of administrative innovation leads via institutional organisational change to the rise of a new class. Chandler starts with emergence of the 'modern business enterprise' and the 'where, how and why [such] an enterprise once started continued to grow and to maintain its position of dominance'. He describes how the development of organisational structures and techniques and the development of professional cadres of managers allowed these enterprises to prosper and grow

> in those industries and sectors whose technology and markets permitted administrative co-ordination to be more profitable than market co-ordination. Because these areas were at the centre of the American economy and because professional managers replaced families, financiers or their representatives as decision makers in these areas modern American capitalism became managerial capitalism.[16]

In this way, institutional change undertaken for internal reasons produced in the longer term a qualitative change in the power structure of modern America and the dominant 'new class that managed it'.[17] The arrival of a certain type of large-scale administrative structure at the level of the firm is accompanied by a social/institutional transformation. The aggregate of these transformations brought managerial capitalism to the USA by 1950.

The picture presented by Chandler in *The Visible Hand* is of a dynamic response by US corporations to US market conditions. In a subsequent book, *Scale and Scope*,[18] he contrasts the different capitalist dynamics of the USA, Germany and the UK. The general tenor of his argument is that UK and German efforts did not measure up to the USA seen as an ideal type. The relevance of this conclusion for a historian of UK developments needs careful analysis. The point at which US practice presented itself as superior, as opposed to merely different, was not as apparent to contemporaries as it is to Chandler.[19] Take, for example, the competitive impact of US corporate practice on the UK in the period before the First World War. Chandler does not find it difficult to show that the activity of UK firms in many of the industries of the Second Industrial Revolution were sporadic and small scale compared to US firms. The latter were clearly positioning themselves in a way that would bring great competitive advantage in due course. This was not particularly apparent to UK industry, nor does it seem to have been any conscious strategy on the part of US firms. Indeed, US competition in the industries of the Second Industrial Revolution appears to have raised little contemporary interest. A great deal more heat was generated by the (largely German) competition which impinged largely on traditional major industries of the UK (textiles, iron and steel, ship-building) and the debate was very largely in terms of free trade versus protection.[20] The debate on US competitive advantage prior to the First World War is thus almost entirely retrospective.

This was not the case by the end of the Second World War. The intervening period marked by wars, booms, slumps and protectionist regimes strengthened and weakened national economies and their firms in different ways. By the end of the Second World War, the 'audit of war'[21] and the superiority of US materiel and organisation were evident and the explanation brought back by UK delegations,[22] and put forward by government enquiries,[23] was particularly focused on the quality and capacity of US management. The UK response immediately post-war was, not unnaturally, focused on the higher output or productivity that such management could achieve: national finances were tight, manpower was scarce and reconstruction and exports were a desperate necessity. It was the shock of the competitive advantage of US firms in European markets after the formation of the Common Market in 1958, however, that forced an examination of the revolutionary nature of US management from a European perspective. J.-J. Servan-Schreiber in *The American Challenge* attempts to set out the essential features of 'an art of *organisation* that is still a mystery to us'.[24]

There are a number of key factors. Servan-Schreiber identifies first a new mode of integration of processes of research, development, production and marketing. Marketing was relatively new in Europe, but it is the mutual reflexivity of the processes that is the key point. A US executive is quoted as saying:

If a German manager wants to increase his production, he studies all the factors that go into the manufacture of his product. But if I want to increase production, I add to these same calculations our research and market predictions so that I will know not only *how* to produce but how to produce the desired quantity at the lowest cost. What interests me is my profit margin. What interests my European competitor is a factory that produces. *It isn't the same thing.*[25]

A second key factor is constant innovation, the major source of profit. A third key factor is the combination of large size, central strategic control and flexibility. Servan-Schreiber says that in consequence

wealth and power are no longer measured in material terms. They are not gifts of nature or chance, like oil or gold or even population. Rather, they are victories won by the human mind: the ability to transform an idea into a reality through the industrial process; the talent for co-ordinating skills and making rigid organisations flexible.[26]

The picture we are presented with, then, is revolutionary forms of organisation and business technique which permit a step change in productivity, profitability and adaptability. These organisations, even if they might not be said to control the market, at the very least shape it by forecasting and innovation. Servan-Schreiber goes on to say that such organisations cannot emerge without a democratic, non-elitist political culture with a highly educated workforce. In other words, the US corporation, the assembly of organisational form and technique, is a cultural creation with its roots in Yankee democratic individualism and optimism which Europe is urged to replicate.

A similar point is made by Harold Perkin though he does not focus on the primacy of the USA but rather on the capacity of metropolitan or first world societies to make a third social revolution (the Neolithic and Industrial Revolutions being the first and second.) This third social revolution 'is, like its predecessors, a revolution in human organisation. At the heart of it is a further rise in manufacturing productivity parallel to the rise in agricultural productivity in the Industrial Revolution'.[27] Just as efficient agriculture had then enabled a minority of the work-force to produce enough food to release the majority for industrial and other work, so now the appliance of technology by skilled management to manufacturing has meant that a minority of the work-force produce consumer goods. This leaves the majority free to provide services of many kinds, but crucially 'the sophisticated services which have transformed human life'. These knowledge-based services like the advances in manufacturing 'are the province of professional experts, without whom they would not exist'.

> It is . . . not the technology that matters but the human skill and social organisation which lie behind it. In other words, it is the professional experts who have constructed the system which in turn has created them. And among the professionals most responsible, the key players are the professional managers of the great corporations and their counterparts in government, the state bureaucrats. They stand at the apex of the new society, controlling its economy and administering its policies and, increasingly, distributing the income and arranging its social relations.[28]

This new society Perkin calls 'professional society',[29] to emphasise the centrality to the new dispensation of applied higher-educated knowledge and those who apply it. The growth of the institutions which the professionals created during the twentieth century meant that 'they grew in power and influence until they were in a position to take over, not by confrontation or violent revolution but by seduction and infiltration – as, indeed, the capitalists had taken over from the landowners before them',[30] and created the third great social revolution. We will examine these ideas for their explanatory power below, but it is worth unpacking Perkin's ideas a little more to place them in the context of the others we have considered above.

For Perkin Big Government and Big Corporation are seen as parts of the same process, both made possible by the social surplus created by manufacturing productivity. The bulk of Perkin's book is a set of accounts of six contrasting first world countries which *interalia* set out the different distributions of power and divisions of labour between state and corporation. The 'professionals' in this account are not greatly different from the 'managers' in James Burnham – both are essentially seen as a global rising class analogous to the bourgeoisie – though the element of class conflict is replaced by serviceable seduction in Perkin. Both accounts, whether explicitly or by implication, describe a class intentionality or will to power. This contrasts with Chandler in both *The Visible Hand* and *Scale and Scope*: in the former the managerial revolution *is* the revolution in productivity, rather than its consequence, and in the latter because the different modes of professional society in first world countries are different versions of the same thing rather than failures to attain the USA's one best way. But at the heart of Perkin's analysis is the understanding that at the heart of the third social revolution lies the invention of organisational structures and techniques which allow a step change in productivity and social control. It was this that gave the competitive advantage which drove the process forward.

We can suggest in conclusion to this section that it is in the invention of the new 'technologies' of organisational structure and control technique and the ramifying institutional change that originated and depended on them which is the 'quintessence of managerialism', rather than the shifts in ownership which so fascinated earlier writers.

Models of the managerial revolution and theories of institutional change

We will now attempt to appraise the different models of institutional change presented by these different definitions of the managerial revolution with particular reference to the UK. The geo-political model presented by Burnham and Rizzi suggests that the managerial revolution is made by a managerial revolutionary class. This model is drawn straight from Marx's ideas on class succession and the release of productive forces.[31] Essential to Marx's model is the concept of new forces developing *within* the constraints of an established social system. At the level of the business organisation, this is a very difficult concept. Businesses are systems of power and internal opposition is not tolerated except within carefully controlled confines. The rhetoric of empowerment in its various historical manifestations has not actually involved the transfer of power. Labour has been able to negotiate its price but rarely the mode of organisation. So while the outside pressures on a business organisation through competition, through various forms of state pressure, from changes to input and output prices, etc., will force attention on the issue of adaptation and change, the decision to change may be arrived at though conflicts among elites but not by internal rebellion.

We might raise the possibility of at least ideological managerial opposition within the firm or among managers as a class, even if the prospect of a managerial revolution made by managerial revolutionaries is dismissed. The idea is not entirely far-fetched. It is possible to see quasi-Saint Simonian tendencies in some of the writing of the 'engineers revolt', Veblen and others at the end of the First World War and echo again after the Second World War and the later work of Berle.[32] These sources are explicitly linked by C. Wright Mills to Burnham's *Managerial Revolution*.[33] The dominant theme in such writings is that what industry required was the primacy of neutral experts (i.e. salaried managers) who could stand aside from the conflict between capital and labour and make decisions for the benefit of the community as a whole. The theme certainly found sympathy in some Fabian writings in the UK.[34] The extent to which such thoughts found expression, let alone influence within large UK businesses, is unknown, but no trace has been found so far by this writer.

We have considered the proposition that separation of ownership and control is the sole motor of the managerial revolution and have concluded that it may be a symptom or a necessary condition, but cannot be a sufficient condition for the managerial revolution. There are also specific UK-based reasons for finding the separation of ownership and control an unlikely motor of institutional change. In the UK, the institutional form that this separation took left company directors with a small percentage of total shareholding as self-perpetuating oligarchies at the top of the largest public companies. I have set out elsewhere the nature and consequences of 'the proprietorial theory of the firm' in the UK which was well established by the end of the nineteenth century and set the scene for much of the development of UK companies in the inter-war years.[35] In brief this theory which can be found instituted in company case law, accounting assumptions, financing principles and company structure asserted the rights of 'the proprietors' (i.e. the shareholders in a joint stock company) in a particular way. A sharp line was drawn between the directors (seen as partial owners representative of the owners as a whole) and managers (seen as employees). Firms were viewed as sets of operations carried out by employees, but initiated and supervised by directors in a manner analogous to the separate roles of politicians and civil servants. (Indeed, it is possible that the theory of the firm and the theory of public administration may have had common roots.)[36]

In other developed economies it seems to have been far easier for boards of directors to have evolved from committees of owners into the highest tier of management, or to have become less powerful 'supervision boards'. In the UK the reservation to the directors of overall co-ordination combined with a strong sense of the board's role and prerogatives led to a fixity of structure and management style which had two broad consequences at the level of the firm. First, firms did not evolve managerial hierarchies much beyond the departmental or functional level, top management being sparse or non-existent, with management technique in consequence being generally under-developed. Second, firms could not easily grow beyond a certain size or complexity of operation or respond dynamically to changing business conditions.

The firms which are being described here were the largest firms in the UK. The restrictions on their development were not those described by the 'institutionalists' like those authors gathered by Elbaum and Lazonick in *The Decline of the British Economy.*[37] The institutional constraints of a market co-ordinated economy did not apply much at all to the early twentieth-century railways, joint stock banks, cotton thread oligopoly or steel/shipbuilding/armaments conglomerates and so on. Such organisations were not without their own innovations, but they tended to remain at the departmental level. The kinds of managerial structures, management information and accounting systems, business planning and budgetary control systems which had been pioneered in the USA in the nineteenth and early twentieth centuries, and would become pervasive there between the wars, were complementary elements of a new holism, a new paradigm of the firm. This paradigm was hardly congruent at all with the model of the firm envisaged by the proprietorial theory. It was not particularly easy, say, to institute and operate a budgetary control system without a top management initiated, cross-departmental annual planning round and management and accounting information feedback loop.[38] Yet the establishment of such a structure effectively established a level of co-ordination below the level of the board that required either a new and demanding executive role for directors, the board effectively becoming top management, or an empowered top management that would inevitably reduce the power of the board. It was the former development that finally emerged in the UK, but it was not until the last quarter of the twentieth century that the process was complete.[39]

The proprietorial theory of the firm was not a theory of 'Personal Capitalism' in the sense of owner-managed or family-controlled firms.[40] There was an undoubted strong element of company director nepotism and 'hereditary management' in UK joint stock companies,[41] but this was the consequence rather than a cause of the privileges of directors. Chandler's use of the term seems to imply a personal choice was made by company leaders, but for many the structures appear to have been almost pre-ordained. Alternatives were barely mentioned and where they were it was usually only to demonstrate the inevitability of the conventional. Long after the real capacity of shareholders in general meeting to check the wide powers and ill-defined duties of directors had disappeared, the legal fiction was that the directors represented and were accountable to shareholders. The result was that the proprietorial theory of the firm became a convenient fig leaf for the largely unrestrained activities of a largely self-serving body of men and in consequence enjoyed considerable longevity. The separation of ownership and control in the UK produced a long-lasting intermediate form of business structure which was not only not managerialist but a prophylactic against managerialism.

Chandler's *Visible Hand* sets a model for organisational change where, if markets allow, firms grow, adopting organisational structures and managerial techniques to cope with the difficulties of growth and internalising transactions as this becomes cheaper than buying in the market. These techniques allow further growth to further serve the market and so on round a virtuous circle. This account of growth and change by administrative logic misses out some very relevant aspects of US management history like anti-trust, crises caused by over-capacity in the depression after the First World War or desperate attempts to rationalise organisations assembled for opportunistic, monopolistic or even megalomaniac reasons.[42] Most importantly for our purposes, however, it assumes that new types of organisation and new managerial techniques are market-expansion driven, a necessary, almost determined, rational entrepreneurial response to market opportunity.

This is unsatisfactory in a number of ways. The idea of a market as a thing 'out there', that pulls productive effort in a specific direction, is almost as much a 'descending analysis' as Foucault calls it,[43] as, say, the Marxist presumption that such and such a historical development took place because it served the interest of the bourgeoisie. It presumes a wider economic intentionality in the market in the same way that Marxism presumes a historical intentionality in the bourgeoisie or proletariat. There are difficulties too with the idea of internal transactions becoming cheaper than transactions in the market. What is meant by a transaction here and what is the extent to which an internal and an external transaction are comparable? And how significant a factor in the growth of firms is the internalising of transactions in any case? Let us take three scenarios. 1) If single-operation firms vertically integrate then internal and external transactions would be comparable: an example might be textile spinning, weaving, finishing and wholesaling firms coming together as a single enterprise. Here, an appraisal of the relative cost advantage of this arrangement over the previous market co-ordination can be made easily. 2) This is not possible when there is no obvious market in which a single operation firm can buy or sell so that if an enterprise is to exist at all it must carry out all operations from raw materials to finished product. 3) The situation is different again when, for example, a horizontal merger aims at monopoly or oligopoly and the reduction of capacity: here costs may reduce through optimum use of plant which may require some modest increase in management capacity. The transactions with the last and next positions in the supply chain have not changed, there is still buying and selling, and the relative contribution to competitive advantage of cost reduction or market hegemony is very difficult to disentangle.

From the cases presented by Chandler, the development of the large firm in the USA owes a great deal to scenarios 2) and 3). It is not at all clear in Chandler's work that any case is made for the primacy of the internalisation of transactions as the motor of managerialism. It appears, in fact, that a more general point may be inferred: that the US economy, culture and society enabled management capacity to grow quickly to an extent where the market, understood in the neo-classical sense, was pre-empted or superseded. Globally speaking, the transactions that it might have been necessary to make in the market to achieve economic ends were not necessary because alternative managerial means had been developed to achieve the same ends which, it turned out, were cheaper. Such a formulation appears to better reflect real developments than an attempt to explain, say, the success of the Ford production line by comparing it with some notion of a putting out system of comparable scale. The reason why managerial hierarchies succeeded was that they did things differently, not that they did the same things better. It is in the demonstration of the nature of this difference rather than the explanation for its appearance that Chandler's scholarship is most helpful.

From our discussion of Chandler's work we can, however, derive a key factor for the development of managerialism, namely, managerial capacity. That is to say, quite explicitly, that the market did not call the managerial enterprise into being by demanding successive incremental administrative innovations as mass production responded to growing market. Rather, the administrative innovations were already available to rationalise the difficulties faced by organisations in varying degrees of crisis in a period of recession. The history of the multidivisional company, on the evidence of Chandler's own work, starts in the post-First-World-War slump of the 1920s. That it could be founded at that point, however, depended on a pre-existing managerial capacity. What, then, are the origins of this capacity that enabled the development of a US 'science of organisation' which eventually so dazzled Servan Schreiber and the metropolitan world in the 1950s? As we have seen, Servan Schreiber rooted the business innovations of US firms in a democratic individualist culture. There is some support to be found in a 1960s debate on the relative inventiveness of the UK and USA in the nineteenth century pitched largely in economistic terms,[44] but which recognises some cultural differences. These cultural differences have been emphasised by later works like R. R. Locke and (by implication) Wiener.[45] And this applies equally to the non-technological organisational and management accounting inventions in the USA. We have the example of the early managerial pioneers on the US railroads and elsewhere discussed by Hoskin and Macve.[46] Innovations in processes and management technique on some railroads and Springfield Armoury are traced back to a new administrative/disciplinary ideological mindset brought to these companies by managers trained at West Point, which was influenced in turn by developments in the Revolutionary French Army. Whatever their importance as sources for later developments, they were ideologically not market-driven. In Chandler's view the innovations these managers brought to the railroads were redundant as far as the contemporary requirements of general railway administration were concerned:

> the innovations made by the early large intersectional roads in organisation, accounting and control went beyond mere necessity. The railroads could have operated well enough with only rudimentary organisational structures. . . Indeed, many roads continued to operate for many years in an ad hoc informal way.[47]

Similarly, Hoskin and Macve discuss attempts by the Waltham Watch Company to mass produce watches. Ultimately successful and profitable, the technical and managerial problems were great and the expense was almost ruinous. The authors sardonically remark that this throws some doubt 'on the viability of the theory . . . that successful organisational transformations are the result of the rational, comparative calculation of transaction costs'.[48]

A further example of surplus management capacity may be found in the work of F. W. Taylor. Again, we have the invention of sets of techniques and an ideology of labour control which have become the norm.[49] Their origins were obsessional and driven. The early experiments were not obviously blessed with success and were accompanied by labour strife. The full Taylor system appears to have cost as much, if not more, in overheads as it saved in extra labour effort.[50] Yet its ambition to have management control every particle of the work process is at the heart of the metropolitan world we live in now. Similar arguments can be advanced in relation to management accounting techniques such as the cost accounting system of Alexander Hamilton Church: here too inventiveness preceded utility.[51] A considerable number of US businessmen were clearly prepared to invest in significant levels of managerial/technical excess capacity. That this investment was to pay off in the longer run because of the human capital it created is undoubted, but it preceded the response of firms to the market rather than being created by firms in response to the market. Seen in this way the creation of the managerialist organisation seems more like the adoption on a new large scale and in a new coherent and systematic way of forms and techniques originally developed in an entrepreneurially contingent and almost existentialist manner. Such developments can hardly be explained by theories of the separation of ownership and control or expanding market-driven development. A much closer approximation may be found in the work of Michel Foucault.

Institutional and societal change in the work of Michel Foucault[52]

Michel Foucault (1926–1984) was not a business historian, nor was he a historian of individual organisations. His field was – though he and his followers appear to dislike the term – the history of ideas and his most significant work for our purposes is his history of the prison published in English as *Discipline and Punish*[53] and the associated collection of essays and interviews published in English as *Power/Knowledge*.[54] In these works Foucault traces, inter alia, the inter-dependent development of the systems of *ideas* and the accumulation of organisational *techniques* that made prisons possible as the principal mode of punishment in the West in the nineteenth century. Foucault does not view this history in narrow institutional terms, however. He shows that the systems of ideas and organisational techniques that made the prison possible were those that underpinned the development of other disciplinary organisations: armies, factories, hospitals, schools. He also proposes that this set of ideas and techniques privileges the social groups that deploy them, and taken as a whole shifts the way society as a whole is conceived of and controlled. We can see, therefore, that there is clear potential to apply this formulation to those changes in institutions and society loosely grouped under the heading of 'the managerial revolution'. Here too the issue is one of the deployment of systems of ideas and organisational technique and the concomitant shifts of social power. We will develop some possible tools after a more detailed look at Foucault's arguments.

Foucault contrasts the theatrical and immensely physically cruel punishments of the eighteenth century condemned criminal with the silent and hidden processes of the 'great uniform machinery of the prison' put in place in the early nineteenth century.[55] The move from one to the other was rapid – less than twenty years – and he seeks to understand how this came about. The origins of the social aspiration which led to the prison system had long-standing roots in systems of state and church surveillance and the disciplines of civil emergency, but were given a new orientation by the 'projects of docility that interested the eighteenth century so much'.[56] Examples were the meticulous time-tabled routines in reformatories, the intricate 'dressage' required of soldiers in parades or manoeuvres and the developing procedures and record-keeping in armies and hospitals. What typified these developments was 'an uninterrupted, constant coercion supervising the processes of the activity rather than its result'.[57]

> What was then being formed was a policy of coercions that act upon the body, a calculated manipulation of its elements, its gestures, its behaviours ... A "political anatomy", which was also a "mechanics of power" was being born; it defined how one may have a hold over others' bodies, not only so that they may do as one wishes, but so that they may operate as one wishes, with the techniques, the speed and the efficiency that one determines.[58]
>
> The 'invention' of this new political anatomy must not be seen as a sudden discovery. It is rather a multiplicity of often minor processes, of different origin and scattered location, which overlap, repeat, or imitate one another, support one another, distinguish themselves from one another according to their domain of application, converge and gradually produce the blueprint of a general method ... On almost every occasion they were adopted in response to particular needs: an industrial innovation, a renewed outbreak of certain epidemic diseases, the invention of the rifle or the victories of Prussia. This did not prevent them from being totally inscribed in general and essential transformations ...[59]

Foucault then sets out in considerable detail methods by which discipline was imposed in a number of institutional settings through divisions of labour, drill, timetabling and precise systems of command. He shows how trained obedience was obtained through conditioned reflex, through examination and record keeping, and how new theories and systems of surveillance were established:

> Hierarchised, continuous and functional surveillance may not be one of the great technical 'inventions' of the eighteenth century, but its insidious extension owed its importance to the mechanisms of power that it brought with it. By means of such surveillance, disciplinary power became an 'integrated' system, linked from the inside to the economy and to the aims of the mechanism in which it was practiced. . . The power in the hierarchised surveillance of the disciplines is not possessed as a thing, or transferred as a property; it functions like a piece of machinery. And although it is true

that its pyramidal organisation gives it a 'head', it is the apparatus as a whole that produces 'power' and distributes individuals in this permanent and continuous field.[60]

It is clear that Foucault is operating at a very high level of generalisation and considering very much more than the history of one institution. What is being set out here are the developing general ideological and technical capacities of society in a particular period which, as well as many other things, make the prison as a total institution both desirable and possible. It was now ideologically and technically possible to apply powers continuously to a whole social body 'which the classical age had elaborated in specific relatively enclosed places . . . whose total implementation had been imagined only at the limited and temporary scale of a plague stricken town'.[61] Technically, mechanisms had been found which made the application of total power efficient. Foucault remarks of one approach that what had been achieved was 'a functional mechanism that must improve the exercise of power by making it lighter, more rapid, more effective, a design of subtle coercion for a society to come'.[62] This description can also be applied to other technical developments he describes as 'the disciplines'. These 'disciplines are techniques for assuring the ordering of human multiplicities'.[63] They allow firstly 'the exercise of power at the lowest possible cost' (whether economic or political), secondly 'the effects of this social power [brought] to their maximum intensity', thirdly and in consequence technical functional structures become at the same time power structures.

In a word, the disciplines are the ensemble of minute technical inventions that made it possible to increase the useful size of multiplicities by decreasing the inconveniences of the power which, in order to make them useful must control them. A multiplicity, whether in a workshop or a nation, an army or a school reaches the threshold of a discipline when the relation of the one to the other becomes favourable.

If the economic take-off of the West began with the techniques that made possible the accumulation of capital, it might perhaps be said that the methods for administering the accumulation of men made possible a political take-off in relation to the traditional, ritual, costly, violent forms of power which soon fell into disuse and were superseded by a subtle, calculated technology of subjection. In fact, the two processes – the accumulation of men and the accumulation of capital – cannot be separated; it would not have been possible to solve the problem of the accumulation of men without the growth of an apparatus of production capable of both sustaining them and using them; conversely, the techniques that made the cumulative multiplicity of men useful accelerated the accumulation of capital.[64]

There are some intriguing resonances here. There is an almost Coasean take on the transaction costs of imposing power. There is an almost Chandlerian sense of the developed technical capacity of large powerful organisations allowing them to grow and become more powerful. There is a 'marx–ish' (though not Marxist) view of accumulating capacity and take off, and indeed specific reference to Marx is made in the text.[65] But there are some key differences. In Foucault's model the techniques predate their use by 'multiplicities', their initial scope is small, being designed to address niche specialist issues.

The gradual production of 'the blue print of a general method' is a process of generalisation, trial and error and speciation. Unlike Marx or Chandler, there is no sense of intentionality, no thrusting bourgeoisie or entrepreneurial strategist arranging a new world or a new structure for themselves in the midst of the old. Indeed, Foucault remarks that the techniques of power were

> [s]mall acts of cunning endowed with a great power of diffusion … They are the acts of cunning, not so much of the greater reason that works even in its sleep and gives meaning to the insignificant, as of the attentive "malevolence" that turns everything to account. Discipline is a political anatomy of detail.[66]

And as the language used makes clear ('cunning', 'malevolence'), there is not only no class intentionality there is no sense of human progress either; there is simply a different mode of social dominance.[67]

Another key difference between Foucault and Marx or Chandler follows from the lack of intentionality and is the nature of social transformations. Clearly, there comes a time when the assembly of niche functional or institutional specialisms become a 'general method', where one mode of social dominance is replaced by another. The way this comes about does not appear to be a major concern of Foucault's and it could be said that he implicitly assumes that the new mode of social dominance simply crystallises out of the possibilities established by 'the disciplines'. Put another way, the prison system simply came about because it was intellectually and practically possible. We should perhaps try and unpack this concept to a greater degree than Foucault does. His historical method from his earliest works up to *Discipline and Punish* had been to let the sources speak and to use exegesis rather than interpretation to set out the structure of thought of a historical period in all its 'otherness'.[68] As a result, through Foucault's work we can see the changes in historical thought and track the different historic senses of what is socially possible. Foucault acknowledges that social and political conditions pose problems – the success of a foreign rival in war, the increasing social dysfunctionality of crime – and that solving these problems requires shifts in social thought and social practice. But while the upshot in terms of the invention of a general institution like a reformed army or the prison is clear, it is much less clear how any aggregate of institutional changes leads to changes in 'general method'. In other words, though he will not say them, how do we know when institutional changes developed contingently and separately develop sufficient critical mass to make a social revolution? In the absence of some spectacular marker like a political revolution, how do we know when some decisive shift has taken place? The answer from Foucault appears to be that we can only recognise such a shift by having little regard for splashy events and concentrating on the mode(s) of public thought and the shape of institutions.[69] We may remark, however, that change appears more likely in conditions of threat or crisis in Foucault's account.

There is also a passage, however, where Foucault suggests that a notional 'History of Detail' in the eighteenth century which would start with '[t]he meticulousness of the regulations, the fussiness of the inspections, the supervision of the smallest fragment of life . . . should bring us, at the end of the century, to the man who dreamt of being another Newton. . .'.[70] This Newton of Detail is Napoleon Bonaparte who 'did not discover this world [of details]';

> but we know he set out to organise it; and he wished to arrange round him a mechanism of power that would enable him to see the smallest event that occurred in the state he governed; he intended, by means of the rigorous discipline that he imposed, 'to embrace the whole of this vast machine without the slightest detail escaping his attention'.[71]

In other words, the small-scale contingent techniques of power can snap into a self-sustaining large-scale system of power as the result of an individual (or group?) will to power as well as a form of self-assembly. The consequence in the former case is an assertive new codification of power, a new generalised ideology and a radical diffusion of techniques of dominance. In both models of change, however, revolutions become revolutionary *after* the fact of power. By extension the 'ideological roots' and 'productive forces' said to have led to such revolutions are simply retrospective rationalisations. A new regime may or may not be sustainable, and this may be a lot to do with the extent or capacity of techniques of dominance available to it, but the will to power comes first. Furthermore, while tools may be adapted and extended by a new regime, they are on this model not called into existence by it. If a change in the mode of social power crystallises from the possibilities established by 'the disciplines', then the will to power can be the seed crystal.

Institutional change and the managerial revolution in UK business

In considering the managerial revolution in the UK I have shown elsewhere[72] that not even the most 'advanced' large business organisations in the UK were managerialist by 1939. I have also shown that on a number of measures understood as diagnostic tests (the defeat of labour, organisational form, managerial recruitment) the managerial revolution was complete in the UK by the later 1980s.[73] A key task for the business historian, therefore, is to explain how such a deep-rooted system changed to the domination of managerial corporations we see around us now. There has been a managerial revolution, but the outcome is curiously at odds with the declared intentions of many of the major players. We appear to have arrived at this position as the upshot of state socialisation and other *dirigiste* measures, sets of shifts and adaptations of firms to desperate circumstances, 'Thatcherite' attempts to restore the primacy of the market and the explosion of City mergers and acquisitions activity. In short, we appear to have had a revolution by accident.

In order to explain how it came about we not only need to know how the essential elements of this accidental revolution were assembled, we need to establish what these essential elements were. We also must ask how the process may, in retrospect, be said to have started. This also relies on the nature of the essential elements of the managerial revolution. What were the elements of structure and technique that could be assembled into coherent systems, where did these elements come from, how did the process of assembly start?

We should be in little doubt that the difficulties were great. We have seen in our discussion of the proprietorial theory of the firm above that there were embedded interests which structurally tended to preclude the take-up and deployment of the elements of managerialist structure and technique in the UK. It is not that initiatives were absent:

UK examples can be found of proto-managerial accounting and other techniques,[74] but the structures in which they were used and the uses to which they were put continued to be for the most part resolutely proprietorial.[75] In the wider world too there was no shortage of visible handles which a visible hand could have turned, had it existed. The major US texts of scientific management and management accounting and US technical journals were available in the UK and there seems to have been a well-established tradition of visits between the USA and the UK by businessmen engaged in similar sectors – examples include railway companies, ICI, Lever Brothers and Herbert Austin. Contacts were also made through cartel arrangements, patent sharing and overseas subsidiaries. There were also UK-based writers on management and management accounting. There were therefore no physical barriers to the transfer of managerial and accounting technique into UK business. The barriers were structural: structures of power and structures of thought.

These structures proved remarkably difficult to break. It can be argued that even the power of the British State could not achieve this directly, despite the post-Second-World-War interventions of nationalisation, anti-trust[76] and the Industrial Reorganisation Corporation (not to mention the pre-war initiatives in steel and cotton).[77] These interventions are best understood as a last resort of the state in the face of disastrous under-performance by UK industry. There were successes (e.g. GEC) matched or surpassed by failures like the collapse of the UK car industry. Both relied on the organisational resources within the firms involved. The central role of Weinstock at GEC is well known. The process of change in the UK car industry, according to Wisler, involved an increasingly difficult search for managements of 'successful' companies to shoulder the burdens of the sector:

> The constancy of strategy was a consequence of the evolution of personal management and the merger pattern of a 'healthy' firm joining with a struggling but not prostrate company. Management of the senior partner ironically adopted the strategy of the junior partner on the assumption that superior management not rationalisation and integration could revive the ailing firm. Of course the, the systems and control needed to consolidate the firms did not exist. The 'better managed' firm was not necessarily better managed but smaller in scale, which was compatible with personal management institutions. The new larger firm soon developed problems similar to those that undermined the original partner.[78]

The nationalised railways, too, continued the agenda of pre-nationalisation management for many years.[79] The syllogism that was clearly assumed to apply at the time was that there were large companies that were competitive and successful; UK companies were too small and not very competitive; therefore, if these UK companies were amalgamated, they would make a large company that was successful and competitive. However, experience revealed that management capacity is the pre-condition for successful operation and growth; size is not the pre-condition of management capacity.

The question, then, is whether management capacity can be ordained from outside? Can it be consciously brought into existence? Our reading of Foucault suggests that the management skills that needed to be institutionally embedded required both practical application and development in a way that privileged and advanced the people that had mastered these skills. This combination of technical skill, organisational utility and career opportunity Foucault calls *Power/Knowledge*. In other words, the social pecking order needs to shift somewhat to achieve the deployment of skills that, in retrospect, appear to be collectively required to achieve some substantial shift in 'general method' and a more general shift in social power relations. Some broad implications appear to flow from this: firstly, an inelastic social pecking order provides little nourishment in the way of implementation, status or career for new skills; secondly, the historic existence of a job title or paperwork showing that some skill was present means little unless, and until it is established how the skill was deployed and micro-social relations affected; third, the supply of skilled personnel does not stimulate a demand for that skill. All these formulations are practically relevant to UK business history. This suggests a general rule: increases in management capacity combine new skills with changed power relations.

How do the ideas of Michel Foucault apply to change in individual businesses and the managerial revolution in businesses generally in the UK? We may summarise our discussion as follows: we have concluded that the invention of new organisational structures and control techniques are at the heart of the social transformation which managerialism represents. We have seen how this managerial revolution in its earliest manifestations is not carried out intentionally by managerial revolutionaries, but arrives because there is excess management capacity which can be mobilised at a time of crisis. The innovations which this crisis management generalises give competitive advantage and establish a pattern that others can follow. Indeed, this competitive advantage can be the external threat or crisis that spurs others to action. The excess management capacity which can be mobilised is not market-driven, but it is the product of inventive ambitions for control sometimes ideologically, sometimes personally obsessively, driven. There is remarkably good fit between these conclusions and Foucault's account of institutional change. His propositions allow us to make sense of some business phenomena that are hardly touched upon by market-driven or class-intentionality explanations, including the origins of large firms, changes in markets, success and failure of companies and so on. Foucault's account is supported against others by certain counter-examples in the UK experience. If, for example, change in organisations is market expansion-driven, then the boom of the 1950s should have transformed UK enterprise. It did not. Less straightforwardly, increasing world competition from the 1960s should, on the face of it, have provided the crisis which led to change if the Foucauldian model is correct. That there was change ultimately is indeed the case, but it was a desperately long time in coming. The crucial missing element, however, was excess management capacity. Foucault's account of institutional change only deals with success – in the sense that something is formed which is the consequence of some critical mass of discrete contingent developments. The obverse, the lack of crucial elements of technical and organisational capacity leading to failure, should apply by extension and appears to do so. The work of Foucault, therefore, appears to set the terms for an important research agenda for the managerial revolution in the UK.

Notes

1 J. Burnham, *The Managerial Revolution* (Penguin, 1962). Originally published New York in 1941.
2 B. Rizzi, *The Bureaucratisation of the World* (Tavistock, 1985). Originally published in French in 1939.
3 A. A. Berle and G. C. Means, *The Modern Corporation and Private Property* (Macmillan, 1932).
4 A. D. Chandler, *The Visible Hand: The Managerial Revolution in American Business* (Belknap, 1977).
5 A. D. Chandler, *Scale and Scope* (Belknap, 1990).
6 J. -J. Servan-Schreiber, *The American Challenge* (Pelican, 1969). First published in French in 1967.
7 H. Perkin, *The Third Revolution – Professional Elites in the Modern World* (Routledge, 1996).
8 See e.g. C. W. Mills, 'A Marx for the Managers' in his collection of essays *Power Politics and People* (OUP, 1967).
9 'It is of the essence of revolutions of the more silent sort that they are unrecognised until they are far advanced. This was the case with the so-called "industrial revolution" and it is the case with the corporate

revolution through which we are at present passing'. Berle and Means, *Modern Corporation*, Preface, p. vii.

10 There is a very substantial literature. There is an extensive bibliography in J. Scott, *Corporations Classes and Capitalism* (Hutchinson, 1985).

11 T. Nichols, *Ownership Control and Ideology* (George Allen, 1969).

12 A. A. Berle, *Power without Property* (1960).

13 R. Dahrendorf, *Class and Class Conflict in Industrial Society* (1957).

14 R. Marris, *The Economic Theory of 'Managerial Capitalism'* (1964).

15 Chandler, *Visible Hand* (as fn 4).

16 *Ibid.*, p. 11.

17 *Ibid.*, p. 497.

18 Chandler, *Scale and Scope* (as fn 5).

19 See the contrasting accounts in R. Morris, *Railroad Administration* (1910) and W. R. Lawson, *British Railways, A Financial and Commercial Survey* (Constable, 1913). The discussions in both are along the lines of pros and cons of the different approaches. In the UK context adventurous capacity was not necessarily commercially successful: see e.g. British Westinghouse (J. Dummeler, *1899–1949* (Metropolitan-Vickers Electrical Company, 1949), p. 28 ff.).

20 It is the traditional staples which feature in E. E. Williams, *Made in Germany* (Heinemann, 1896).

21 C. Barnett, *The Audit of War* (Macmillan, 1987); idem, *The Lost Victory* (Macmillan, 1995).

22 'Practically every Productivity Team which has visited the US is agreed that productivity per man year is higher in the US than Britain. They attribute this mainly to two factors'. The first is effort. 'Second there is a quality in management [stimulated] in particular by that part of [higher education] devoted to administrative studies'. *Productivity Report: Education for Management* (Anglo-American Council on Productivity, 1951).

23 'We cannot escape the conclusion that there is in the United States a massive equipment for training future managers, incomparably greater both in volume and depth of experience than anything which has been contemplated in Great Britain. That fact in itself is bound to have a progressively adverse effect on our competitive position'. Ministry of Education, *Education for Management* (HMSO, 1947).

24 Servan-Schreiber, *American Challenge*, p. 22.

25 *Ibid.*, p. 20.

26 *Ibid.*, pp. 45–46.

27 Perkin, *Third Revolution*, p. 6.

28 *Ibid.*

29 Perkin's two earlier major works, *The Origins of Modern English Society 1780–1880* (Routledge, 1969) and *The Rise of Professional Society* (Routledge, 1989), provide histories rich in allusive detail but in a theoretically uncertain framework. The word 'professional' carries considerable sociological deck cargo of which Perkin appears largely unaware. In any case the word is used in different senses in each of the three works. In *The Third Revolution* 'professional' in the sense of self-managed qualification, self-regulation and trained independence of judgement is now more or less at odds with his actual subject of study, senior corporate managers and state bureaucrats.

30 Perkin, *Third Revolution*, p. 5.
31 'In the social production of their life, men enter into definite relations . . . of production which correspond to a definite stage of development of their material productive forces. . . At a certain stage in their development, the material productive forces of society come in conflict with the existing relations of production or – what is but a legal expression of the same thing – with the property relations within which they have been at work hitherto. From forms of development of the productive forces these relations turn into their fetters. Then begins an epoch of social revolution'. K. Marx, *Preface to the Contribution to the Critique of Political Economy* (1859).
32 C. H. Saint-Simon (1760–1825) believed that the crisis of modern society could be solved by the social dominance of a quasi-religious order of scientific savants. For the 'engineers revolt' E. T. Layton, *The Revolt of the Engineers* (1986); P. Meiksins, 'The "Revolt of the Engineers" Reconsidered' in T. S. Reynolds (ed.), *The Engineer in America* (University Press, 1991); T. Veblen, *The Engineers and the Price System* (1921). For the corporate citizen in a corporate society, E. F. Cheit (ed.), *The Business Establishment* (John Wiley, 1964). A. A. Berle, *Power without Property* (1959).
33 Mills, *Marx for the Managers*.
34 S. Webb, *The Works Manager Today* (Longmans, 1918); A. Albu, *Management in Transition* (Gollancz, 1942).
35 J. M. Quail, 'Proprietors and Managers: Structure and Technique in Large British Enterprise 1890 to 1939' (unpublished PhD thesis, University of Leeds, 1996); J. Quail, 'The Proprietorial Theory of the Firm and its Consequences', *Journal of Industrial History*, 3, 1 (2000).
36 T. L. Alborn, *Conceiving Companies* (Routledge, 1998) shows just how politically ideological the structures of UK companies in the early nineteenth century were with 'shareholder republics' consciously set against 'old corruption' cronyist businesses.
37 B. Elbaum and W. Lazonick (eds), *The Decline of the British Economy* (Clarendon Press, 1987).
38 Interestingly, however, some individual proprietors found it possible to introduce systems with the true character of budgetary control – W. H. Lever and Herbert Austin. See J. Quail, 'More Peculiarities of the British: Budgetary Control in US and UK Business to 1939', *Business and Economic History*, 26, 2 (Winter 1997).
39 J. Quail, 'Mapping the Managerial Revolution in the UK – Definitions, Dating and Demonstrations' in *Proceedings of the Conference on Business History and Theory* (Centre for Business History in Scotland, 1999).
40 The phrase 'personal capitalism' is used by Chandler as a general explanation for UK industrial failure and its meaning is often stretched far beyond the meaning proposed here. See the remarks of L Hannah in his review of *Scale and Scope* in *Business History*, 33, 2 (April 1991).
41 J. Quail, 'From Personal Patronage to Public School Privilege: Social Closure in the Recruitment of Managers in the United Kingdom from the Late Nineteenth Century to 1930' in A. Kidd and D. Nicholls (eds), *The Making of the British Middle Class?* (Sutton, 1998).
42 An alternative reading of *The Visible Hand* indicates that the reorganisation at Du Pont at the end of the First World War was caused as much by the need to deal with a much expanded business faced with a slump in

64   *John Quail*

demand for munitions as anything else. General Motors was assembled by a shopping spree by W. C. Durant using others' money as well as his own which ended in crisis and the departure of the founder. The reorganisation was crisis management rather than long-term strategy. The strategy actually made sense of the structure. The structure and management of the oil companies following the break up of Standard Oil by anti-trust appears to have the response to competitive pressure rather than market expansion.

43   M. Foucault, *Power/Knowledge: Selected Interviews and Other Writings 1972–77* (ed. Colin Gordon) (Harvester, 1981), p. 99ff.

44   H. J. Habakkuk, *American and British Technology in the Nineteenth Century* (CUP, 1967); S. B. Saul (ed.), *Technological Change: The United States and Britain in the Nineteenth Century* (Methuen, 1970).

45   R. R. Locke, *The End of Practical Man* (1984); M. J. Wiener, *English Culture and the Decline of the Industrial Spirit* (CUP, 1981).

46   A useful summary of their work and ideas may be found in K. W. Hoskin and R. H. Macve 'Knowing More as Knowing Less? Alternative Histories of Cost and Management Accounting in the US and the UK', *Accounting Historians Journal*, 27, 1 (June 2000).

47   Chandler, *Visible Hand*, p. 120.

48   Hoskin and Macve, 'Knowing More', fn. 53.

49   H. Braverman, *Labour and Monopoly Capital* (Monthly Review Press, 1974).

50   Judith A. Merkle, 'The Taylor Strategy', *Berkeley Journal of Sociology*, 13 (1968).

51   As displayed in the Hans Renold company in the early twentieth century. See the remarks of C. Renold in D. Solomons (ed.), *Studies in Costing* (Sweet and Maxwell, 1952), p. 29.

52   What follows is only a summary of part of Foucault's thinking. While care has been taken not to do violence to the meaning of the text no claim is made of a comprehensive survey of the two works discussed. Foucault's work is extraordinarily wide-ranging and subtle with breaks over time in subject matter and approach. And if Foucault's work is diverse, then the purposes it has been put to by others are even more so.

53   M. Foucault, *Discipline and Punish: the Birth of the Prison* (Penguin, 1979). Published as *Surveillir et Punir* (Gallimard, 1975).

54   Foucault, *Power/Knowledge* as fn 43.

55   Foucault, *Discipline and Punish*, p. 116.

56   *Ibid.*, p. 136.

57   *Ibid.*, p. 137.

58   *Ibid.*, p. 138.

59   *Ibid.*, pp. 138–139.

60   *Ibid.*, pp. 176–177.

61   *Ibid.*, p. 209.

62   *Ibid.* The invention was the 'panopticon' proposed by Jeremy Bentham as a model for prisons where all the prisoners could be observed from a central tower. This has great symbolic power for Foucault. See the discussion in *Power/Knowledge* under the title 'The Eye of Power'.

63   Foucault, *Discipline and Punish*, p. 218. 64. *Ibid.*, pp. 220–221.

65   *Ibid.*, p. 221. Foucault's relationship with Marx is interesting. He had spent some time in the French Communist Party and his contempt for that kind

of Stalinist Marxism was total. Yet he was clearly attracted to the passionate Marxism of his students in Tunisia and the post-1968 Maoist Group, Gauche Proletarienne. He confesses in *Power/Knowledge* to have included passages from Marx in his work without attribution to see whether anyone spotted them!

66 Foucault, *Discipline and Punish*, p. 139.
67 See e.g. 'The Eye of Power' (as fn. 62) where Foucault asks whether matters would be much improved if the position of the prisoners and warders was reversed.
68 This is most densely illustrated by Foucault in *The Order of Things* (Tavistock, 1970). Published in French 1966.
69 There are problems of method here, however. Whose thought is 'public'? In 1928 Pitman published its *Dictionary of Industrial Administration*, edited by John Lee. It has been recognised by both contemporaries and more modern commentators as an extraordinary piece of work, gathering as it did best practice from the USA and UK. It sold very few copies. It was magnificent but it was not normal practice – normal thought and normal practice being the key test.
70 Foucault, *Discipline and Punish*, p. 140.
71 *Ibid.*, p. 141 (quoting Treilhard).
72 Quail, 'Proprietors and Managers'.
73 Quail, 'Mapping the Managerial Revolution'.
74 See e.g. T. Boyns and J. R. Edwards, 'British Cost and Management Accounting Theory and Practice *c.* 1850–*c.* 1950; Resolved and Unresolved Issues', *Business and Economic History*, 26, 2 (Winter 1997); see also Quail, 'Proprietors and Managers', p. 99ff.
75 There were a few notable exceptions, Hans Renold Limited being perhaps the best examples.
76 See H. Mercer, *Constructing a Competitive Order* (CUP, 1995).
77 See the contributions of Stephen Tolliday and William Lazonick in Elbaum and Lazonick, *Decline of the British Economy*.
78 T. R. Whisler, *The British Motor Industry 1945–1994* (OUP, 1999), pp. 89–90.
79 T. R. Gourvish, *British Railways 1948–73* (CUP, 1986).

3 The evolution of education and training in British management consultancy*

Michael Ferguson

Formal training for management consultants has a history that dates back as far as the mid-1920s in Britain, but consultancy itself has a longer antecedence, with its birth embedded in the industrial situation of the mid-nineteenth century. This mismatch between the commencement of consultancy and that of formal training for consultants is directly related to three separate, but linked factors. These factors are the structure of management consultancy during its early years, the individuals involved in the delivery of those services, and the type and scale of the services provided by those pioneer consultants in Britain. These factors will be briefly covered in this introduction by way of an outline description of the first fifty years or so of the history of British management consulting; that was the period in time of the first phase of management consultancy education and training in Britain (for a graphical representation of these phases see Figure 3.1).[1]

The commencement of management consultancy services in Britain occurred at a time when there was a general recognition that Britain was no longer leading the world in terms of technological development, manufacturing and trade. Apart from factors relating to competition from abroad in terms of overseas and domestic markets, one aspect of this scenario was the way in which businesses were being managed. In the consultancy context initially, this was to do with the financial dealings of the enterprise. Two editorial articles in *The Engineer* in 1867 and 1869 highlighted some of the deficiencies in the British industrial milieu of the nineteenth century.[2] Both of the articles focused on the lack of expertise of consulting engineers in obtaining accurate costs, or even the processes from which costings were derived. Part of the reason for this was that the consulting engineers passed on

DOI: 10.4324/9781003206996-3

| Pre-Education and Training Phase | 1869–1925 Free Lance Consultants – Professional Background | | |

| On-the-Job Training Phase | 1926–1941 On-Site Training – Bedaux and Others | | |

| Off-Site Training Phase | 1941–1960s Off-Site Training – Big Four | | |

| Specialisation Phase | 1960s–1990s – Business School Training | 1960s–1990s – Specialist Training | 1960s–1990s – Professional Training |

| Current, Mixed Phase | 1990s–Present – Mixed Model | | |

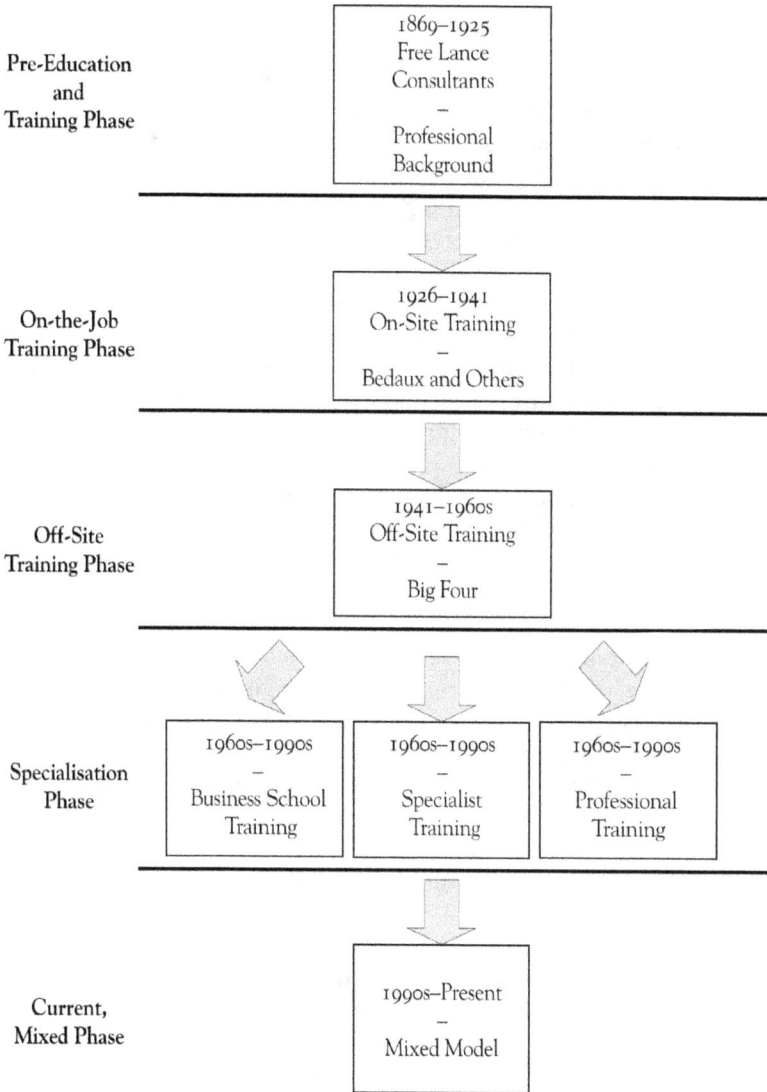

Figure 3.1 Phases of education and training.

this responsibility to the manufacturers and this generally resulted in sloppy and inaccurate estimates. It was probably no accident, therefore, that the first identified instance of a management consulting service occurred at about the same time in 1869. That service was provided by a chartered accountant, Montague Whitmore, of Clerkenwell Green in London, who was at the time acting as a full-time consultant. Whitmore's service was advertised in *The Engineer* in 1869 under the title 'Avoid Losses and Failures', with the substance of the service related to a cost management system for installation into factories and engineering workshops. Also, at that time a number of other accountants provided similar services on a part-time basis when work in their own area of professional expertise was going through what could be described as 'quiet periods'.[3] This has prompted some to comment that this was the beginning of the development of management consultancy services within accountancy firms, although it was not until after the Second World War that there was any real movement in this direction.[4]

Management consultancy services during the remainder of the majority of the nineteenth century were orientated towards the financial aspects of businesses in a consulting environment that was made up of a range of individuals from a professional accountancy background. Training for consultants was non-existent, other than some professional accountancy training, services were generally provided to small and medium-sized businesses, primarily engineering and manufacturing firms, and the makeup of services was based entirely on the consultants' own design and antecedence. In other words, consultant services were by and large extensions to contemporary accountancy practices, albeit in areas such as cost accounting that lay outside of the main thrust of auditing at that time.

Changes to the makeup and delivery of services occurred at the end of the nineteenth century with the appearance of production efficiency as a second major strand to management consulting.[5] Some consultants at the turn of the nineteenth century and beyond linked financial services with production planning and control as a means of improving productivity within firms; these were largely engineers with an appreciation of the financial aspects of the business and experience in the operational processes within the workplace.[6] During the second and third decades of the twentieth century other forms of services began to appear, specifically services in salesmanship, sales promotion and publicity, and in the employment of financial and operational information in the management decision-making process. However, throughout the history of management consulting until the mid-1920s a number of common factors dominated consultancy.

Consultants were freelance, the overwhelming majority came from a professional background in either accountancy or engineering, most had professional qualifications, the services they provided were largely of their own design and none had received any training in consultancy. The majority of these consultants maintained links with their professional associations through the writing of papers and the delivery of lectures concerning their personalised techniques of consultancy.

In terms of the corporate consultant strength in Britain by the mid-1920s, their numbers were probably no greater than twenty full-time consultants and that would have represented their maximum numbers at any one time. Also at the time, and for many years afterwards, the dominant ethos in business was that 'managers are born, not made' and this limited consultancy services to the operational aspects of firms.[7] At the same time, during this first fifty years or so of consultancy, there was in Britain no real culture of business and management training and, therefore, consultants had nowhere to go to extend their knowledge of business practices and techniques.[8] For ease of reference within this article, this period prior to the mid-1920s will be known as the 'Pre-Education and Training Phase' of management consulting.

Therefore, for the first fifty or so years there was no culture of consultancy training in Britain, nor indeed from a business perspective would there have been justification to establish such a centralised culture with a relatively small handful of consultants practising their trade. Education and training occurred inside the established professions, not outside of them for practising consultants, and training in business and management had yet to be established as a cornerstone of the educational system in Britain. Therefore, in Britain there were no facilities for consultant training.

The purpose of this article is to describe the evolution of training for management consultants, an important and influential group within business and management circles that have had, and continue to enjoy, a disproportionate impact on the way that organisations function. This article charts the progression of training and development from the beginning of consultancy when consultants plied their services with little more than their professional background to prepare them for their work, through a range of corporate methodologies that can be represented by five phases of development that bring us up to date with today's situation. The introduction has described those corporate beginnings when consultancy primarily evolved from the accountancy profession, but all that changed in the mid-1920s with the arrival of the Bedaux company in Britain in 1926.

This article focuses on the phases of development of management consultancy education and training; a number of distinct phases are identified and described, and for ease of reference these phases are entitled:

Pre-Education and Training Phase.
On-the-Job Training Phase.
Off-Site Training Phase.
Specialisation Phase.
Current, Mixed Phase.

I. The first consultant training (On-the-Job Training Phase)

Consultants from Charles E. Bedaux and Company first appeared in Britain in 1923 for the purpose of conducting an assignment at the British subsidiary of an American company, the Eastman Kodak Company.[9] This, as it later turned out, partly inspired the founder to set up a permanent operation on British soil in 1926. In terms of this article, the importance of the Bedaux company is concerned with its general philosophy in terms of its consultant selection process and its modus operandi with regard to consultant training.[10]

In the mid-1920s in Britain there was no dearth of availability of suitably qualified individuals available to take up appointments as management consultants in a newly formed company. The introduction to this article bears witness to this. The employment policy of the Bedaux company at that time took account of this fact and sought potential consultant recruits based on a set of clearly defined requirements. Individuals had to demonstrate their fitness to become a consultant by showing that they had a professional background with professional qualifications; most of the early consultants with Bedaux were engineers, experience in the practical aspects of management, and a good educational background, usually at university level. In addition, they were subjected to an interview in which they had to demonstrate their potential competence to become a consultant.[11] Unsurprisingly, the majority of consultants at that time were in their thirties when they first entered consultancy as a career, a necessary outcome when antecedence is taken into consideration.

Because of this selection regime in terms of employing individuals with what was considered to be an appropriate background and because the services offered by Bedaux had been developed in-house, the Company deemed it necessary only to train new consultants in the techniques of consultancy, the core functions of the Bedaux approach at that time. There were two strands to the Bedaux training strategy. Firstly, all new consultants were provided with a copy of Charles Bedaux's book, *Industrial Management*.[12] The book was unusually written in that it was in the context of a poorly performing company. This style was used to highlight Bedaux's model of his 'eight principles of industrial efficiency'. It was these principles in combination that lay at the heart of the Bedaux service and was the focus of the training regime.[13] Secondly, using the book as the standard, a period of on-the-job training (between six and twelve weeks) was carried out with an experienced consultant until the trainee could demonstrate his competence to conduct assignments on his own. I use the word 'his' because at that time consultants were male and it was probably not until the late 1930s at the earliest that the first female consultant appeared in Britain. On-the-job training consisted of six core subjects: time and motion study, analysis sheets and routine reports, base rate analysis and reference periods, relaxation factors, process allowance and normal working time, study of indirect workers and B values, and the composition of setups.[14] Throughout the period of training, the trainee had to submit to Head Office in London a weekly report describing the activities carried out during the week. At any time during the course if, in the opinion of the trainer, the trainee could not be brought up to an acceptable standard then training was discontinued.[15] The first training course in Britain commenced in September 1926. The trainee was Norman Pleming and the experienced consultant (trainer) was Frank R. Mead, the then managing director of the British operation.[16] Pleming's training was carried out during the first assignment for the new company at the British Goodrich Rubber Company Limited at Leyland in Lancashire.[17]

Whilst the development of this particular strategy to consultant training was a positive step forward at a time when nothing else was occurring in that field, there were four main problems with this approach. Firstly, assignments were ad hoc in terms of the makeup of services and it was, therefore, impossible to gain a balanced grounding in the techniques of management consultancy and in the range of environments to which they were applied at that time. Unlike today when many consultants specialise in a particular industry, the concept of sector specialisation was not applied within Bedaux at that time. Secondly, this particular methodological approach to training necessitated the availability of an experienced consultant and this meant that during the first few years the Company could only effectively cope with a small number of new recruits at any given time. Often experienced consultants were regarded as those who had completed their training and were deemed experienced enough to conduct assignments on their own. Thirdly, partly as a consequence of the second problem and partly due to a relatively rapid expansion in terms of the number of assignments conducted, training was sometimes shortened when the volume of demand for services required the availability of greater numbers of trained consultants. This meant that operational considerations were sometimes more important than an effective grounding in the techniques. Finally, not uniquely a problem associated with the Bedaux approach but one that should be considered with this type of training more generally, the previous experience of the trainer consultants was inevitably mixed and the Bedaux regime was not developed to cope with that contingency. Therefore, whilst there was the appearance of a standard, in reality none existed.

The weaknesses to the training regime identified above were clearly recognised by the British operation and this set in motion the development of a new training strategy. Other factors also played a role, and these were also instrumental in forcing change to the general approach to training. Of these other factors, two stand out as being particularly important. The first of these related to the general acceptance of Bedaux operations at the shop floor level, both in terms of operatives and in some quarters with regard to supervisory staff, in those firms where the techniques were applied. By the end of the decade some of the consultancy assignments were beginning to come up against organised unrest and this did little to enhance Bedaux's reputation.[18] At the heart of some of these assignments were criticisms of the Bedaux approach, specifically in relation to little regard being paid to consultation at all levels within the firm. The second factor was concerned with the number of new recruits to the Company that increased at a pace that the old regime could not cope with because the demand for services was beginning to outstrip supply. From an initial strength of two in 1926, consultant numbers increased to forty by the end of the decade. Therefore, because of these factors and the weaknesses identified above, the Company put into place a new training regime in 1930.

The 1930 consultancy environment in Britain was still in an embryonic stage of development in terms of organised consultancy practices; it still consisted of no more than twenty or thirty freelance consultants, a new British management consultancy called Harold Whitehead and Staff, formed in the previous year, and the Bedaux company itself.[19] The Bedaux company was still the leading provider of productivity services and principal innovator in terms of consultancy training. In 1930 the Company developed a manual for staff training, refined further in 1934 and given the title 'Training Course for Field Engineers'.[20] The stated purpose of the training was three-fold: to ensure complete instruction in everything an engineer should know prior to assignment, to present this instruction in such an order as to be most readily assimilated and to avoid too comprehensive instructions before students' general fitness has been confirmed. The training course was in eight parts: the first part was carried out at the Head Office of the Company and remaining seven were in the field under the direct instruction of an experienced consultant.[21] Those eight parts between them provided the necessary information and covered the skills required to conduct assignments using the Bedaux method at the time:

Part 1 – Head Office instruction, including basic administration.
Part 2 – The practical application of work-study techniques.
Part 3 – The use of analysis sheets and the development of routine reports.
Part 4 – The application of base rate analysis and reference periods.
Part 5 – The application of relaxation factors, process allowance and normal working time.
Part 6 – Factors in relation to indirect workers and the development of 'B' values.
Part 7 – The composition of setups.
Part 8 – Special applications and final instructions.

Each part of the course was concluded with the trainee taking a formal test to demonstrate his competence to continue on to the next phase; the structure and detail of the testing regime was also prescribed within the training manual. The testing regime provided the Bedaux company with a number of opportunities to re-assess the fitness of the trainee to continue as a potential consultant with the Company. Successful completion of the training, however, meant that individuals became formally known as 'Bedaux Engineers'. In the United States, but less so here, this mark of competence was almost an industry standard at that time. In fact, there were a number of reported incidents of Bedaux imitators in the United States who only really came to light when their assignments failed and their true antecedence became known.[22]

One glaring omission within the 'manual' was any reference to consultation at all levels or any other suggested methodology to bring organised labour into the consultation process; one of the main criticisms made of the Bedaux approach in Britain at that time. In addition, training still relied heavily on the personal skills of the 'experienced' consultant and these would have varied between individuals.

Nevertheless, while these negative aspects were present within this approach to consultant training, there were four main advantages that this particular strategy had over its predecessor. First, it provided for a structured approach to training. It was a standard course, prescribed in detail within the training manual. Second, each phase of the training had to be successfully completed before individuals could move on to the next and this may have resulted in repeat applications of the work until the standard had been achieved; there were no prescribed time limits with regard to the duration of the training. Third, there was an objective assessment of fitness at each stage with Head Office monitoring progress through the submission of the test papers for marking. Trainees that failed to meet the prescribed standards were not considered fit for employment as consultants. Finally, because each phase had to be completed, it was often necessary for training to be carried out in a number of working environments in order for trainees to complete their course; therefore, there was greater opportunity for trainees to gain some grounding in different industrial environments.

After the first few years in the 1930s, in the same year (1934) that Bedaux revised its training manual, two new consultancies were formed by disillusioned ex-Bedaux consultants.[23] At least one of these consultants, John Leslie Orr, left Bedaux service for reasons associated with the development needs of consultant personnel within the Company. From his perspective, the erosion of the quality of service during the late 1920s and early 1930s was a direct result of a policy of rapid expansion in terms of the number of new inexperienced consultants within the Company with a system of training that failed to meet the exacting development needs of those men. This was a point made in the previous section in which the pre-1930s regime could only cope with a small number of consultant trainees and rapid expansion in numbers, as was witnessed towards the end of the 1920s, resulted in the erosion in the quality of training delivered. There was, according to Orr, a direct correlation between the training of consultants and the standard of service provided by them, a correlation that remains true today.

The two new consultancies adopted a similar approach to consultant training to that of Bedaux through on-the-job training.[24] However, there the similarities ended at time when interest in management consulting was beginning to spread across of range of industries, including some elements of the service sector. The first of these companies, Production Engineering Limited, (P-E) developed its on-the-job training regime through an approach that concentrated on analytical techniques, work-study, production control, and report writing and presentation.[25] In parallel with this, and from an operating standpoint, the Company's philosophy extended to that of ensuring that during every assignment at least two trained consultants were always responsible for the task, one of whom was a more senior man. This was reflected in the motto of the Company 'duo melius uno', translated to mean two heads are better than one; but the growth rate for P-E in the pre-war period in relation to operating consultants, whilst relatively steady, was slow in comparison to the other consultancies at that time. A number of the new consultants into the Company were ex-Bedaux employees, already trained in the techniques of consultancy, and these factors meant that there was very little pressure on the Company to raise its training regime to a more formal level. This became a phenomenon of the post-war period.

The other company formed in 1934, Urwick, Orr and Partners Limited, at the very beginning of its history had a stated aim to '... select, recruit and train suitably qualified and experienced men as consultants'.[26] To achieve that aim, and because the demand for services necessitated expansion of the Company in terms of its consultant staff, on-the-job consultant training was also developed. In a similar vein to Bedaux, and because some of the new consultants already had experience in consulting, the recruitment policy of the Company meant that only men with a suitable management experience and professional background were considered for employment; therefore, training in the consultancy techniques of the Company was the main focus. Nevertheless, because it was Company policy to make every effort to shed the negative image of management consultants at that time, emphasis was also given to the softer aspects of consulting, specifically those that related to communication at all levels when at a clients' premise.[27] For the first time the concept of profession underpinned the approach to consultant training, reflected in a point of policy at the outset for Urwick Orr: 'To exercise the highest possible professional standards of conduct'.[28]

Each consultancy believed that it would gain greater market share if it could demonstrate that its services were professional, and more comprehensive and effective than its competitors. It was believed that to achieve that aim, effective consultant training was a necessary prerequisite. However, during this period the range of services provided was still largely occurring in manufacturing firms and most were based on production efficiency, even though other types of services were beginning to be developed. In other words, work-study remained the main analytical weapon in the consultants' armoury and this provided a point of concentration in terms of the delivery of training. Where other forms of services were being developed or pioneered, specialist practitioners were employed with a background in the areas concerned. What was about to change in terms of the delivery of training was the principle that training should be solely conducted on the job; the period of the Second World War brought with it innovation in terms of the point of delivery and the beginnings of off-site consultant training.

II. The beginnings of off-site training (off-site training phase)

During the period of the Second World War, little changed in terms of training in business techniques in Britain and although some initiatives had been put in train in the previous period by a small number of professional bodies in the engineering field, these were put on hold until the cessation of hostilities. At the start of the War consultant training was still carried out on the job in the techniques associated with work-study, but by that time one or two leading companies, for example ICI, had developed their own in-house regimes for work-study practitioners. By 1940, the work of management consultants had been recognised as an important contribution to the war effort and consultancy had been declared a 'Reserved Occupation' by the Government within strict guidelines.

In 1941, William Lodge, a former Bedaux consultant, who was at that time employed by Urwick Orr, resigned from his post and set up the first off-site consultancy training school for work-study in Bedford.[29] Lodge was an older man who did not wish to continue as a consultant under the pressures of wartime service. The title 'school' may seem somewhat grandiose by today's standards in the light of its size and appointment because it was set up in the living room of Lodge's house. Nevertheless, it did become known as the Bedford Work-Study School. This was a private enterprise scheme, run by Lodge himself, and did not come under the direct control of Urwick Orr, although the Company was the principal customer of the School at the beginning. Urwick Orr used the facilities of the School for initial consultant training and for the training of other consultants who did not have a work-study background. Other than directly providing training for consultants, the primary importance of the school lay in two distinct areas. First, it established the principle of consultant training away from the clients' premises; revolutionary at the time when on-the-job training also provided some economic value for the consultancy company at little or no additional cost through the trainee's involvement at the client site. And, secondly, it partly provided the inspiration for the introduction of management training schools run by the consultant companies in the period after the War. This is discussed later in this article.

Lodge initially developed a course of three weeks' duration in work-study and base rate analysis for six participants at a time. Using in-house workshop techniques for the preliminary stages of the course, it had a practical component through arrangements with three local factories in the Bedford area. The effects of utilising local factories had a number of consequences. Firstly, it engendered co-operation between both the School and consultants with local companies in the Bedford area, through raising the awareness of efficiency techniques and broadening the consultant-industrial network. Secondly, it spread the utilisation of work-study techniques into participating firms, which otherwise may not have used such methods, through the provision of free consultancy services. Ordinarily these firms may not have been fully aware of the benefits of such techniques or have been able to afford consultancy services at the time. Finally, it provided training facilities in work-study, when vacancies existed, for personnel of the co-operating firms. These facilities were later opened out to a broader customer base as an open commercial venture. After the War, the course at Bedford was extended to eight weeks and the course content then included labour cost control, material cost control, planning, costing, cost control, methods improvement, time standards, factory layout, work flow and operational performance standards. By the time it closed its doors in 1961, it had trained 650 students from industry in addition to the volume of training it provided to consultants.

In the first decade and a half after the Second World War significant changes were occurring in management consultancy in Britain. The wartime experience had demonstrated the value of consultant services in a range of environments within industry, commerce and government. Throughout those fifteen years, the range of services provided by management consultants began to expand at an unprecedented rate in comparison to the whole history of management consulting previously. The corporate structure of consultancy had evolved to witness an industry dominated by four major consultancies (commonly referred to as the 'Big Four'), a small number of accounting companies that had set up consultancy arms, the embryonic beginnings of specialist consultancies (including the beginning of IT consultancy), a range of smaller companies and an increasing number of sole practitioners.[30]

On the back of that changing environment, each of the Big Four during that fifteen-year period set up and managed their own schools of management for consulting staff, client personnel and a range of other students from a wide variety of backgrounds.[31] This was an important step forward in terms of education and training for business and management in Britain, at a time when very little else was occurring in those fields more generally in support of those objectives.[32] However important as that contribution was to management education and training, in terms of this article this innovatory movement was significant with regard to the training of Britain's management consultants. Taking each of the Big Four in turn in terms of the date of establishment of their schools, the remainder of this section examines the contribution of these companies to off-site consultant training.

The Bedford Work-Study School and the personal desires of Lyndall Urwick provided the impetus for Urwick Orr to establish a school of management in 1948. This was initially to train consultants in the techniques of consultancy and to provide a broader education in other areas of business and management, precisely in line with the stated aim of the Company reported previously. From the outset, however, client personnel were admitted as students at the School. The 'Slough Training Centre', as it became known, initially provided an eight-week course in work-study and related subjects.[33] Within a short period of time there were a number of specialist options that broadened the scope of training. These options were production, marketing (known at that time as distribution) and finance (known at that time as control); a general management course was added to the curriculum in the mid-1950s. Alongside the School, a workshop was established where the practical skills of work-study could be practised. The school at Slough and the Bedford Work-Study School operated in parallel in the ensuing years.

The major contribution to management training, however, came through the setting up of the Urwick Management Centre that was established at Baylis House in Slough following a conversion programme in 1957–1958. The Urwick Management Centre was formed because the Slough Training Centre became too small to support the demand for providing training services. Its inadequacy stemmed from the fact that it was a listed building and, consequently, the Company was unable to expand the premise. Following in the footsteps of Urwick Orr, in 1953 Associated Industrial Consultants (AIC) set up a 'College of Management' at Dunford College in Sussex for consultant training and client personnel. Later, in 1957, AIC provided training services at Bush House, its Headquarters, moving subsequently to larger premises at Bilton House in Ealing. This became known as the AIC Staff College, but it remained non-residential throughout its history. The staff of the 'College' was made up of experienced consultants of the Company who had received special training and had, according to the Company, an aptitude for teaching.[34] Supplementing the permanent staff, lectures were provided by practising consultants, operational managers and trade union representatives. In addition, some clients of the Company provided historical sketches of the work carried out by AIC. To assist with the delivery of lectures, various teaching platforms were applied: the use of films, models, case histories of actual assignments, management games, seminars and syndicate work.

In a similar fashion to the other major consultancies, P-E trained its recruits in the traditional way on the job during the first decade of its existence. However, during the war years off-job training was developed for two or three major industrial clients. As a logical extension of that experience, in 1953 facilities were developed at Park House at Egham in Surrey for both P-E consultants and client personnel. In parallel to this, training was also delivered at the London Headquarters of the Company at Grosvenor Place. Formal training courses were established making use of the previous experience of consultants in the field. Such training was developed utilising, what the Company considered to be up-to-date management thinking at the time.[35] Similarly, Personnel Administration obtained in 1953 a building suitable for the establishment of a management training centre. Sundridge Park, at Bromley in Kent, opened its doors in 1953 for the purpose of training consultants and managers in short courses appropriate to their roles. As a testimonial to the demand for the delivery of training at Sundridge Park, this school closed its doors only recently, bowing down to commercial opportunities in turning the venue into a conference centre.

The main advantages that these schools had over the previous regime of training was that courses varied in content and were matched more closely to the needs of the individual consultant. Training was more responsive to the changing nature of consultancy work and could be developed through a regime that called upon the collective experiences of the individual companies through case studies, and a range of teaching aids could be employed appropriate to the subject content. However, from the perspective of practical experience, theoretical training alone would not prepare a consultant for working in the operational environment and the school-centred approach could not entirely replace on-the-job induction training; but it did prepare the trainee more effectively to cope with that experience and develop a standard company-wide. It also sent out a clear signal to prospective clients that the major consultancies took seriously the preparation of consultants and were willing to invest in their development before letting them loose in the wider world where inappropriate decisions could have catastrophic consequences within their client organisations.

III. Expansion and specialisation (Specialisation Phase)

The previous section highlighted the situation in the post-war period in which there was both a rapid growth in the number of consultants and consultancies, and an increase in the range of services provided by them. Until the 1960s the majority of consultants and consultancies tended to be generalist in terms of service delivery, providing the whole range of services available at that time. From the 1960s onwards, as that range of services broadened even further and new and specialist forms of consultancies appeared, the then platform of training delivery proved inadequate for all practical purposes. This section describes a period in the history of management consulting in which there was a distinct movement towards specialisation in education and training for consultants, as well as at the same time a continuance of the previous mode of off-site training within the major British consultancies of the day.

The period of the 1960s through to the 1990s was a dynamic period in which consulting reinvented itself through a change in its corporate structure; four principal factors played a role in that change process. Firstly, there was the appearance in Britain of overseas consultancies, largely American, offering services at the boardroom level. This migratory movement was made possible through changing attitudes within British businesses to the managers' role and, as a consequence, the provision of assistance by external agencies in the higher management functions was beginning to become more widely accepted. Secondly, in parallel with this, the major accountancy companies challenged the established generalist consultancy firms, initially in areas that had a financial orientation. Up until the period of the 1960s, the consulting arms of accountancy firms offered consultancy services, largely to their auditing clients, on a much smaller scale, with little or no real impact to the major British firms. Thirdly, new specialisms began to appear on the back of developments in technology, specifically in IT consultancy. These specialisms were largely serviced by the established consultancies within a fairly narrow band of services and by the growing IT industry itself, although the notion that the latter group actually provided management consultancy as part of the IT services function at that time could be open to challenge. Finally, overarching these movements, and from a professional organisational perspective, the Institute of Management Consultants was formed in 1963 as a professional body for individual consultants. This was the first time that individual consultants were represented by a central association, although previously in 1956 a trade body had been formed to represent consultancy firms.[36]

Whilst all these changes were occurring to management consultancy at the corporate level, the British generalist firms were expanding their individual portfolios into those areas also serviced by the specialist consultancies mentioned above, although within the major British firms the delivery of services was beginning to become more specialised and the true generalist consultant was becoming a rare breed of individual. At the same time, the industry was expanding through the creation of smaller niche consultancies and a growing number of sole practitioners. All of these changes to the structure of consultancy witnessed the beginning of a new phase in education and training from the 1960s onwards. Three distinct movements can be identified, as well as a continuation of the off-site training practices of the major British companies.

The first of these movements was the prerequisite of business school and university education as the standard prior to employment as a consultant by some of the major consultancies, especially those who operated at an international level. This was highlighted by the arrival in Britain from the end of the 1950s of American consultancies led by McKinsey and Company to conduct assignments at the boardroom level of firms. McKinsey brought with it a culture of development that was typified by an education within American business schools. This occurred at the same time that changing attitudes within businesses towards involvement in the strategic decision-making processes opened up new fields for consultancy in Britain. The average starting age of American consultants was less than their British counterparts and a large number had received a business education as their initial grounding in contrast to many of the British consultants who had commenced their careers in engineering and the professions, entering into consultancy at a later stage during their working lives. This was a new concept within Britain; the established principle prior to that was that consultants received their experience of business prior to entering consultancy. The arrival of American consultancies and the business school culture brought with it, what was viewed by many within business and consultancy, a 'cultural elite'.[37] Arguably, consultants working at the very highest levels within client firms would benefit more from a business school background rather than the then traditional entry into consultancy, although some of the larger British consultancies in the 1960s also offered high-level management services without this prerequisite.[38] However, from a British educational perspective, the opportunities to study for an MBA prior to entering into consultancy did not exist until the formation of the Business Schools in London and Manchester during the mid-1960s, and there were only limited places available until the business school culture spread to

82   *Michael Ferguson*

other universities within higher educational institutions.[39] Therefore, in terms of education and recruitment, and personal development, the business school approach was a form of specialisation in its own right, reflecting the need of consultancies to demonstrate that they employed suitably qualified personnel to work within the consulting environment.

More generally, however, specialisation was the result of the broadening of consultancy in terms of the types of services provided, the development of technology that witnessed the growing use of computers within businesses and the arrival of the accountants as a serious challenge to the generalist British consultancies with an initial orientation towards the financial aspects of business. The second movement in education and training reflected this growing specialisation, resulting as a consequence of the broadening of consultancy and a movement away from the previous orientation that centred upon productivity services delivered operationally within firms using techniques such as work-study. Ignoring for the moment financial services that will be discussed in relation to the accountants and the introduction of new technology, three streams of consulting became increasingly important during this whole period. These streams were marketing and sales, human resource management and strategy services. From the perspective of service delivery, specialist consultants in these fields appeared in greater numbers, new consultancies were established that concentrated in these areas, there was a movement into this country of consultancies from overseas (British consultancies also internationalised their services at a greater pace in the post-1960 period) and the generalist consultancies of British origin broadened their service portfolios to accommodate these new services. The lead in these new service areas often came from the major consultancies through internal innovation and developments in management techniques more generally; from a training and development perspective, the whole field opened up so that the range of training providers increased in number and variety.

The management training schools of the Big Four British consultancies widened their curriculums to accommodate these service areas so that the scope and variety of training matched service delivery. There was, however, a physical limit to that expansion and other avenues of training increasingly became important as a means of gaining the necessary skills in order to deliver the range of services on offer at the time. The practical effect of the broadening of services from a consultant perspective meant that individual consultants moved towards specialising in specific areas of consultancy, even within the generalist consultancies, and their training and development needs could be managed more effectively through targeted training in those specialisms.

The universities in Britain, together with further education colleges, became increasingly involved in providing short courses and seminars in general management and other specialist business and management subjects during the 1960s and beyond. Often they provided a means through which consultants could gain the necessary knowledge to assist them in their roles.[40] Privately financed training institutions also played an important role for some consultants wishing to broaden their knowledge and expertise in specialist areas of business and management. During this whole period a growing number of private training schools opened their doors for the delivery of training in business and management subjects, a number of these classified themselves as training consultancies because they also took their services outside of the classroom and some definitively linked recruitment with training.

The new breed of consultants from the accounting companies that began to firmly establish their position in Britain during the 1960s initially had a reliance on their professional backgrounds and professional qualifications, with the orientation of their services being financially based.[41] Some specialist training occurred in the techniques of consultancy and in the soft skills associated with change management. As they broadened their services to encompass other areas of consultancy, then the pattern of training and development mirrored those of the generalist consultancies through the services of public and private education and training institutions.

The 1960s was also the period when information technology began to increasingly play an important role in the delivery of services, initially from a narrow base, expanding to cover most aspects of consultancy by the end of the period.[42] By the 1960s, there was a clear recognition that IT consultants, the majority of whom were specialist management consultants, had a need for training in various aspects of information technology. This need increased as the breadth of service delivery expanded into areas such as software development, information systems design and development, Computer Aided Engineering (CAD/CAM) and robotics as a means of improving production. Whilst initially these specialists came from the established consultancies, or from the niche consultancies specialising in IT services, the growing IT industry itself became increasingly involved in IT consulting. Some internal training was developed within the major consultancies, but because of the specialist and emerging nature of information technology training in its various aspects, some training was carried out by the IT companies themselves, and some was provided by a growing number of specialist training schools. Often the delivery of IT services went hand in hand with parallel services in specialist IT training for clients.[43] Through the process of time, public educational and training institutions also became involved in the delivery of courses in information technology.

The final movement in education and training that marked out the Specialisation Phase was that of the short-lived attempt by the Institute of Management Consultants (IMC) to develop a qualification in management consulting – the development of a baseline standard in core consulting skills for British management consultants.[44] This occurred in the late 1970s as a pilot scheme, with initiation occurring in 1980. One motivation for setting in train a qualification in management consulting was to develop an entry standard for membership of the Institute.[45] The examination was in three parts: Section 1 was concerned with the environment and practice of management consulting,

Section 2 was related to business appraisals and implementing change, and Section 3 dealt with specialisms within consultancy. There were two main problems associated with introducing a qualification and entry standard for consultancy: the universality of the qualification and the fact that it applied to only new members of the Institute. In terms of universality, the title management consultant was, and is, not protected by professional regulation; any one can use it and there is no requirement to be registered with a professional body. With regard to its limited impact, it had only relevance in terms of individuals seeking membership of the Institute of Management Consultants at that time, which represented a minority of consultants operating in Britain. For existing members of the Institute, there was no mechanism in place to ensure that they attained the Institute standard. Therefore, the Institute itself accepted dual standards. This initiative was eventually discontinued and the Institute has searched ever since to find practical ways of standardising entry into management consulting.

What marked out the Specialisation Phase from the other phases was that consultants attended education and training courses, or had a portfolio orientated towards their particular specialist area within consultancy. The main difference between this phase and the previous phases, or the Mixed Phase that followed it, was that there appeared to be a defined stream of education and training associated with a particular mode of service delivery. This was not just-in-time training, a feature of the Mixed Phase, but a distinct orientation towards service delivery within a defined specialism. In summary, four definite streams can be identified that represented the period from the 1960s to the 1990s. These were the continuance of the formal training delivered at the consultant company training schools, with a shift in emphasis towards specialist subjects, the provision of courses in universities and business schools as an entry standard for consultancy and a method of on-going development, specialist training, especially in the newer aspects of consultancy, and the development of professional qualifications to establish a standard within consultancy and to gain admittance into the Institute of Management Consultants.

IV. The present situation (Current Mixed Phase)

For all practical purposes, the situation changed again during the 1990s and the whole model of education and training for consultants became even more mixed, making it difficult to identify a structure or a progressive approach for individual consultants at the corporate level of consultancy. This came about because of a number of factors. The progressive prominence of information technology as the central focus for consulting services meant that the two became inextricably linked and as technology became more complex and broad, so did consulting assignments. This is emphasised by the development and widespread introduction of the Internet as a medium for both communications and training services. The major consultancies, with a history of involvement in information technology that stretched back nearly four decades, were part of that evolutionary process. However, information technology also supported the increasing prominence in Britain of self-employed consultants and small firms, for which service delivery is often only underpinned by the previous experience of the individuals providing that service, largely within niche areas of consultancy.

In parallel with the effects of information technology, and the demands that these bring to consultant training, broader issues on an industry wide basis have also played a role during this period. For example, the increasing globalisation of consultancy services as a number of major consultancies strive towards developing a global market for their service products. Globalisation has brought with it standardisation in terms of service delivery within individual consultancies across its range of locales, and disparity as individual consultancies develop unique packages with similar sounding service titles. The majority of these major consultancies have 'recognised' the importance of recruiting graduates to their organisations, albeit with no real experience of business or finance, and the development of graduate programmes in order to indoctrinate individuals into the consulting culture, or at least the particular version practised by the individual consultancies.

At another dimension, during this period, there has been a direct impact on training through the effects of the waning prominence of professional bodies when compared to the general growth of consultancy, and the lack of influence of these bodies overall in terms of professional standards. The early ambitions of professional institutions to develop industry standards have all but disappeared as individuals within the major firms look towards the firm to provide and set the standard, and determine the individuals' development needs. This has, in part, been made possible through the emergence of non-core consultancy bodies delivering specialist consultancy training in areas where there is no advantage to develop the training skills internally. This has, in turn, led in some measure towards a reliance on just-in-time training to meet specific client needs, resulting in a movement away from consultants developing a broad base of skills. Dealing with each aspect in turn, it is possible to describe a scenario that is both mixed and confusing from a global consulting perspective.

The progressive prominence and expansion of the use of information technology in consulting has meant that a whole range of specialist areas have emerged, and continue to emerge, that complicates the requirement of training for management consultants. Specialist IT consultants, covering a very narrow range of services, have become the norm rather than the exception. Today it is common to see recruitment agencies advertising for consultants in areas that have become so specialised that vacancies could only be filled from a relatively small pool of individuals when compared to the overall size of the consultant force operating in Britain; the training needs of these individuals can also be very specialised and specific to the individual. More generally, because of the link between management consulting and information technology, consultants require a background and training in the techniques of consultancy, the specialist field of activity and a good working knowledge in the application of information technology. Sole practitioners and individuals from smaller firms are less likely to gain that expertise from formal training courses. Larger firms and the global companies have developed a range of measures to accommodate that need. These will be viewed later within this section.

The arrival of the Internet brought with it the opportunity to use its capabilities to deliver training more widely and at a distance for consultants. Some consultancies, for example A. T. Kearney's parent EDS, provide specialist services through e-education strategies to deliver wide-ranging courses in a broadening environment. EDS' e-University facilities and services provide consultants and others with similar needs, with the ability to continue their training wherever they may find themselves at any point in time through accessing the Internet. EDS University's Consulting Competency Centre provides training in the basic grounding of consultancy, as well as providing a digital library of materials.[46] The employment of digital learning strategies, as they are often described, is also used by other major consultancies to satisfy the training and development needs of their staff and clients. The Internet has also brought with it a marketing environment that has been effectively used by training providers and specialist training consultancies to spread the knowledge of their curriculums more widely. This has brought the appearance of greater choice in terms of the availability and variety of courses.

The globalisation of consultancy services and the development of global consultancies have encouraged the use of the Internet and other portable training methodologies within the major international firms. This has had the effect of standardising the approach within consultancies to training and development in the key competences of consulting. There the similarity ends, with each firm developing its own unique approach to training delivery and content. The majority of the major firms, however, teach their version of the principles of consultancy in-house, including marketing and sales.[47] A number of consultancies also provide mentors to transition the new recruits into the consulting mode. Some of these mentors are also career counsellors who provide advice and assistance on the development needs of the individual. Accenture, for example, takes this approach a stage further and has developed a mentoring programme that includes networking between consulting communities within the Company with a view to enhancing professional development and progression. However, corporately within consultancy, specialist forms of training tend to be conducted outside of the firm, unless a particular consultancy is itself a specialist service provider and delivers its own in-house training for its consultants.

Because of increasing specialisation corporately within consultancy, including between the major players, training needs are different within each firm. These needs are satisfied through a network of training providers in the public and private sectors, using a variety of methods, often just-in-time for a consultant. Many educational institutions provide courses at pre-degree and degree level in consultancy and related subjects.[48] A whole range of private training providers deliver courses in the fundamentals of consultancy, including project and change management, and other specialist providers concentrate on specific areas of interest to consultancy. In parallel with this general development in education and training is the increasing prominence towards the recruitment of graduates and the development of graduate induction programmes. For example, the Boston Consulting Group's London programme covers up to two years through a curriculum that includes training in other countries to broaden the experience of the individual. Not all of the major consultancies go to these lengths, but the majority have graduate training programmes, including associate programmes to introduce students at university to various aspects of consulting prior to entering the firm. In general, graduate programmes have a fixed component, consisting of the core skills of consultancy as determined by the individual consulting company, and a variable component, determined by the needs of the client and the individual trainee dependent upon the specific circumstances at the time.

Finally, another trend that has emerged over the last decade in response to the level of growth in consultancy within Britain is that of the initiatives of professional bodies to establish a standard approach to consulting. This is at odds with the general thrust of education and training for consultants, but nonetheless adds to the rich tapestry of opportunities for consultants at the beginning of the twenty-first century. Two main initiatives can be found at the heart of this approach: the 'Certified Management Consultant' qualification of the Institute of Management Consultancy and the 'Certificate in IS Consultancy Practice' of the British Computer Society.

The Certified Management Consultant (CMC) qualification currently awarded by the Institute of Management Consultancy is a competence-based qualification that is recognised in a range of countries throughout the world, primarily throughout the membership of the International Council of Management Consulting Institutes (ICMCI) where it is a defined international standard for individual management consultants.[49] Each consultant who applies for certification must firstly demonstrate that he/she has three-year management consulting experience. Therefore, it is a post-experience qualification and not one that defines entry standards. Successful applicants will have a degree or professional qualification, or an additional five-year consulting experience in lieu, and be a member or owner of an independent practice, or an internal consultant who meets the Institute's independence criteria.[50] The qualification is then awarded to those individuals who either successfully complete a written examination or can satisfy an interview panel that tests the candidate's knowledge of the code of conduct of the Institute and its common body of knowledge. In support of that, the candidate must provide two sponsors who are members or fellows of the Institute, and written descriptions of five assignments with client references that can also verified through an interview process. The CMC qualification is viewed as a positive step forward within professional consultancy circles and is a means of demonstrating that an individual has met certain criteria before an award is made. The obvious drawbacks to such a qualification is that it is more relevant to independent practitioners than consultants in larger firms, the majority of practising consultants are not members of consultancy institutes through which the award is made and the whole process is largely subjective in application.

The British Computer Society's Certificate in IS Consultancy Practice is a new initiative, launched in 2001; the first examination took place in February 2002.[51] There are two entrance routes to gaining the Certificate: standard and direct. The standard route requires candidates to have a minimum of four-year experience in either Information Systems or Information Technology, and be at least twenty-four years of age and attend the course and examination. The direct route requires candidates to have a minimum of three-year consultancy experience and to submit a resume of their experience to demonstrate their competence to attempt the examination only.[52]

In Britain, the Certificate in IS Consultancy Practice is likely to have a greater reach than the CMC qualification, simply because the membership of the BCS is greater than that of the Institute of Management Consultancy and early indications of take up are positive. However, whilst the qualification and course is designed to cover many of the background skills of management consulting, it is in part orientated towards the IT community, or those consultants who provide IS/IT services, and by and large is also a post-experience qualification.

V. Summary and conclusions

The current mixed model has occurred following a long and dynamic period of evolution that has closely matched the delivery of services. The model is confused because on the one hand there are positive attempts by professional bodies to employ a standard in terms of the core skill requirements for management consulting, and on the other what appears to be a scatter gun approach to education and training at the corporate level of consultancy. The evolution of management consultancy education and training has moved through a number of distinct phases, and each phase is marked by a dominant approach, although continuity was as much a theme as change as the older order continued to survive in parallel with each of the new ones:

Pre-Education and Training Phase (1869–1925): The early era of consulting in Britain in which individual consultants developed services based on their accumulated experiences and where training in the techniques of consultancy had not yet been developed.

On-the-Job Training Phase (1926–1941): The period following the creation of consulting companies in which training was linked to the assignment process itself. Consultants were professionally qualified with experience in business and the techniques of consultancy were learnt on the job through skill transfer from a senior consultant to a junior colleague. This was made possible because the range of services was relatively narrow and the dominant methodology was that of work-study.

Off-Site Training Phase (1941–1960s): Through chance circumstances in 1941, the first off-site school was developed at Bedford to provide training in work-study techniques. In the first twelve years of the post-war period, the major consulting companies of the day opened their own training schools for consultants and client personnel. Initially, the training provided was concerned with work-study techniques, together with some general management courses, but as new services were added to the portfolios of the various companies, specialist courses were also developed.

Specialisation Phase (1960s–1990s): Continuation was as much a theme as change during this thirty-year period. The schools operated by the consulting companies continued to deliver courses, but the curriculums broadened as consultancy expanded. Change came about through three separate forces: the arrival of American consultancies providing services as the board room level and consultants with a business school background, the accountancy companies moved into consultancy initially specialising in financial services, and the arrival of information technology and IT consultants with different training needs from those of their generalist peers. In parallel with these movements, there was an aborted attempt by the Institute of Management Consultants to establish a standard in the key skills of consultancy, and the universities and a plethora of other training providers increasingly offered business-orientated courses.

Current, Mixed Phase (1990s–present): The development of the Internet and the explosion of services relating to information technology, inextricably linking consultancy with the new technology, complicated further the training environment for management consultants. Within that environment, the major players developed their own distinct approach to training, particularly in the areas of key skills and graduate training. A plethora of education and training providers deliver courses in a range of specialist and business subjects. The Internet enabled the development of online learning and the creation of e-universities. In parallel with these developments, although somewhat separate, the creation of qualifications by the professional associations associated with management and IT consulting provided other avenues for consultant training. However, a general theme of this phase is the reliance on just-in-time training to meet specific clients' needs.

What the Phases have indicated is that the business of management consulting progressively became broader in context and as a result of those increasing complexities the delivery of education and training for consultants itself became more complex, just in time and attuned to the delivery of those services. There is the appearance of order in that training matched the needs, but there is also confusion because in order to meet those needs consultants have a wide choice of training, delivered by a whole range of providers through a variety of means.

Notes

* This article is based on a bullet point presentation given by the author at the British Computer Society's launch of its Certificate in IS Consultancy Practice on 11 September 2001. The term education is used in this context to loosely describe the direct and indirect involvement of consultants in the higher education process.

1 For a full and up-to-date account of the history of management consulting in Britain, see M. Ferguson, *The Rise of Management Consulting in Britain* (Aldershot: Ashgate Publishing Limited, 2002).

2 The two editorial articles were entitled 'Prime Cost', 8 November 1867, pp. 405–406 and 'The Estimates of Consulting Engineers', 3 September 1869, p. 166.

3 One such individual was Edwin Waterhouse, a founder in the firm of Price Waterhouse in 1865. The work of this man highlights the difficulty of differentiating between some of the services provided by accountants and management consultants during that period.

4 E. Jones, *True and Fair: A History of Price Waterhouse* (London: Hamish Hamilton, 1995), pp. 57–58.

5 Production services remained the core focus for the majority of management consultants until the 1970s and early 1980s in Britain; even today supply chain management is an important area of management consultancy service.

6 A pioneer in this field was Alexander Hamilton Church who developed the concept of production centres and the machine hour rate as a method of apportioning costs within the production environment.

7 J. F. Wilson, *British Business History, 1720–1994* (Manchester: Manchester University Press, 1995), pp. 161–163.

8 For a full account of the provision of education and training for management in Britain, see E. F. L. Brech, *The Evolution of Modern Management*, Volume 5, Education, Training and Development for and in Management in Britain, 1852–1979 (Bristol: Thoemmes Press, 2002).

9 The title consultant had not been adopted at that time, Bedaux consultants were known as 'field engineers' and it was not until the 1930s that
   'consultant' as a descriptive norm began to appear in the nomenclature
   associated with consultancy in Britain.

10 The work of the Bedaux company in Britain is largely remembered in
   publications for its development and application of techniques related to
   work-study and payment incentive schemes. These techniques remained
   the mainstay of consultancy services in Britain within the major consultancies through to the 1970s and 1980s, with subsequent modification and
   improvement to their application.

11 In principle, this remained the applicant standard for the larger British
   consultancies until at least the 1960s.

12 C. Bedaux, *Industrial Management: The Bedaux Efficiency Course for Industrial Application* (Cleveland, Ohio: The Bedaux Industrial Institute,
   revised edition, 1921). British consultant trainees were provided with the
   revised edition, the original was dated 1917.

13 The eight principles were the keeping of records, the establishment of
   standards, planning, the compilation of schedules, the routing and des-
   patching of work, standardisation, graded remuneration according to individual production and standard practice instructions. For a full account
   of these principles, see Chapter 3 of Ferguson, *The Rise of Management
   Consulting in Britain.*

14 The Bedaux approach has often been described as a version of time study
   within the Taylor tradition. Clearly, time was only one element of the approach and there were many differences between the Taylor and Bedaux
   methodologies. This approach later became known as work-study and the
   subjects collectively within the training course made up that methodology
   at that time. Bedaux's methods were distinctive to his mode of operation
   and personalised to represent the Company's involvement. For example,
   the use of nomenclature such as B values was a means of separating the
   Bedaux approach from others at that time. B stood for Bedaux, and values
   were based on a non-monetary indicator of effort and reward. For a fuller
   account of the Bedaux methodology, see Chapter 3 of Ferguson, *The Rise
   of Management Consulting in Britain.*

15 M. Brownlow, *A History of Inbucon* (unpublished historical account,
   1972), p. 28.

16 Mead was not only the managing director, but he was also the only consultant of the British operation at that time, having gained experience within the
   Bedaux company's American operation. Pleming was the first British consultant and he later went on to become the Company's managing director.

17 This was an extension of an earlier assignment carried out at the parent
   company in the United States.

18 During the period at the end of the 1920s and the first few years of the
   1930s, all told eighteen stoppages were attributed to the introduction of
   the Bedaux system within firms in Britain. Other stoppages occurred
   elsewhere in the world involving Bedaux consultants. For an account of
   these, see S. Kreis, 'Toward the discovery of a science of labor: The Bedaux system and British scientific management, 1923–1945' (University of
   Missouri-Columbia occasional paper, 1987) and Chapter 3 of Ferguson,
   The Rise of Management Consulting in Britain.

19 Harold Whitehead and Staff was formed in 1929 specifically to provide services in salesmanship training based on the principles developed by its founder after whom the company was named. At that stage in its history its focus was narrow in scope, but following the completion of its first assignment its orientation expanded to include all the then established aspects of sales and marketing.

20 The training manual was reproduced as an appendix in an account of the history of the Bedaux company in Brownlow, *A History of Inbucon*.

21 In support of the training manual, two other documents made up the trilogy of handbooks for issue to new consultants: 'Code of Practice' and 'Outline of Terms Governing the Remuneration of Engineers of the Company'. Each had a role to play in determining the practice of management consulting within the Company and the relationship between the consultant and the client.

22 M. Brownlow, *A History of Inbucon*, pp. 39–40.

23 The new companies formed in 1934 by ex-Bedaux consultants were Production Engineering Limited (Robert Bryson) and Urwick, Orr and Partners Limited (John Leslie Orr).

24 The reasons why ex-Bedaux employees formed these two consultancies were related to the negatives associated with the Bedaux approach at that time and a wish to expand into other areas of consultancy outside the then Bedaux portfolio. For a fuller account of this phase of the history of management consulting in Britain, see Chapter 4 of Ferguson, *The Rise of Management Consulting in Britain*.

25 P-E, *Fifty Years of Professional Enterprise: The Story of P-E* (London: S. Straker and Sons Limited, 1984), p. 11.

26 Urwick, Orr and Partners Limited, *A Brief History of Urwick Orr & Partners Limited* (new staff induction note number UG/12/6, 1978).

27 As previously stated, the negative image came from the adverse reactions of client personnel during some of the Bedaux assignments in the early 1930s. Specifically, it was reflected in an approach that failed to implement a policy of consultation at all levels and the need to bring along the workforce in the change management process.

28 Urwick, Orr and Partners Limited, *A Brief History*.

29 Lodge had joined Urwick Orr in 1937, having previously been a Bedaux consultant.

30 The 'Big Four' was Associated Industrial Consultants (formerly the Bedaux company and commonly referred to then as AIC), Production Engineering Limited (P-E), Urwick, Orr and Partners Limited (UOP), and Personnel Administration Limited (PA). AIC and UOP were both taken over in the 1980s by P-E and Price Waterhouse respectively, P-E was later taken over by Lorien Consulting in the 1990s and only PA survives today as a major force in management consulting. P-E International is now part of Genus PLC.

31 External students came from industry, commerce, government departments, the public services and the trade unions, as well as a range of other environments in the public and private sectors.

32 For a more detailed account of the contribution of management consultants to the education and training needs in Britain, see Michael Ferguson, 'Models of Management Education and Training: The "Consultancy

Approach"', *The Journal of Industrial History* (Volume 4, Number 1, 2001), pp. 88–112.

33 The Slough Training Centre was initially established on one floor at 17 Mackenzie Street, near the railway station at Slough. Before long, the demand for course places meant that the School had taken over all three floors of the building and the training staff increased from one to five. For a more detailed account of the training provided by Urwick Orr, see G. Sanders, 'The Urwick Management Centre', *Keeping in Touch* (60th Anniversary Edition, Journal of the UOP Keeping in Touch Association, Number 58, July 1994), pp. 10–13.

34 M. Brownlow, *A History of Inbucon*, pp. 82–84.

35 P-E, *Fifty Years of Professional Enterprise*, pp. 17–18.

36 Management Consultants Association (MCA).

37 P. Tisdall, *Agents of Change: The Development and Practice of Management Consultancy* (London: William Heinemann Limited, 1995), p. 73.

38 Today, a number of the major consultancies recruit directly from the universities, looking towards the MBA as only one option in a range of disciplines available. The taking of an MBA is often viewed as a stage in the development process for consultants, a qualification that is useful once a basic grounding in consulting has been achieved.

39 For a full account of the formation of business schools at London and Manchester, specifically Manchester, see J. F. Wilson, *The Manchester Experiment: A History of Manchester Business School 1965–1990* (London: Paul Chapman Publishing Limited).

40 A series of publications produced by the British Institute of Management during the 1950s and 1960s, commonly referred to as *The Conspectus of Management Education*, charts the availability of management and business education throughout that whole period. The final edition of the series, produced in 1968, highlighted the appearance of specialist departments within the universities that often attracted titles such as School of Management and Department of Business Studies, among others. See also Ferguson, 'Models of Management Education and Training', p. 91.

41 Although the major accounting companies began to supply consulting services from the first few years after the end of the Second World War, it was not until about the mid-1960s that they challenged the established generalist firms in any numbers. Increasingly, the supply of consulting services was viewed by many within the accounting profession as being in conflict with the core services of an accounting practice. Initially, this resulted in accounting companies setting up consulting arms or divisions, progressing to the establishment of separate businesses under the same banner and, in a number of cases today, eventually leading to a total separation of their operations.

42 Although IT consultants first began to appear in Britain in the late 1950s with the introduction of services in relation to computer feasibility studies and computer bureau services, the 1960s was the period of their establishment as specialists within management consultancy. Today, it is difficult, if not impossible, to separate out information technology from consultancy, or consultancy from information technology. IT has forced change to consultancy operations and, in the context of education and training, created additional challenges to the education and training of

management consultants. See Chapter 9 of Ferguson, *The Rise of Management Consulting in Britain.*

43 The development of information technology and specialist consulting services also gave birth to recruitment consultancies that wholly or largely specialised in IT personnel recruitment.

44 The Institute of Management Consultants was formed in 1962 with the objective of representing individual consultants and the establishment of corporate standards through a graded membership scheme. The Management Consultants Association, formed earlier in 1956, was the trade body for the industry and only represented consulting firms, not individuals.

45 P. Tisdall, *Agents of Change*, pp. 88–91.

46 The course consists of modules that are described as Consulting Overview, EDS Project Management Methodology, Fundamental Consulting Skills Workshop, Business Process Reengineering, Strategic Planning, Manufacturing Enterprise Leadership, Business Improvement Planning and Elements of the E-Business Solution, and includes a Business Solutions Workshop.

47 The purpose of marketing and sales training as an aspect of basic consultancy skills is that many of the consultancies require their consultants to deliver a minimum level of repeat and new business as a standard objective. This is often linked to career progression and longevity within the firm.

48 For example, a number of educational institutions provide a Master of Science degree in various aspects of consultancy; these include Ashridge Management Centre (MSc in Organisational Consultancy) and the University of Salford (MSc in Management Consultancy).

49 The International Council of Management Consulting Institutes (ICMCI) is a global association of national management consulting institutes. It has a membership that spans across Europe, the Americas, Africa, the Middle and Far East, and Australasia. The ICMCI maintains an international code of professional conduct, an international common body of knowledge, and standards for certification and reciprocity between nations. The national institutes are responsible for administering the CMC qualification according to the defined international standards.

50 Independence is a reference to maintaining an objective approach to recommendations in the best interest of the client.

51 The BCS has been running a Consultancy Skills Workshop over a number of years and is now part of the Professional Development Programme of the Society. The Certificate in IS Consultancy Practice is a continuation of that initiative as a large number of its members come from a consultancy background.

52 For those attending the course, the syllabus is in six parts: overview, management of the client relationship, assignment structure, management and control, management of people and relationships, conducting a consulting assignment and managing the quality of consulting assignments.

4 Marxist manager amidst the Progressives

Walter N. Polakov and the Taylor Society

Diana Kelly

Assumptions of rigid authoritarianism and malign intent to workers have often placed serious limitations on scholarly analysis of scientific management. In recent years, these assumptions have been questioned, as scholars have re-evaluated Taylorism through examination of primary documents and through evaluating the protagonists of scientific management in the context in which they operated. By such analysis, these scholars have shown that the heart of the scientific management movement, the Taylor Society, reflected many of the Progressive ideals that pervaded the first decades of twentieth-century America. Indeed, such was the spirit of critical analysis and debate within the Taylor Society that, while most practitioners and intellectuals who were members of the society were liberals, individuals whose ideological commitments were more radical also belonged to the Society.[1] That an outspoken and avowed Marxist such as Walter Polakov could find a place in the Taylor Society attests to its ideological pluralism.

This paper thus aims to show that far from being an anathema to a socialist such as Polakov, scientific management offered a vehicle which could minimise the deleterious effects on workers in the transition from capitalism to socialism. As has been shown elsewhere, scientific management also offered the opportunity for broader applications at the sectoral and national levels, an aspect well known to many scientific managers. A further objective of this paper is to highlight that investigation of less well-known but active scholar-practitioners emphasises the rich tapestry of ideas, a far cry from the flat portrayals often found in the historical analysis of business ideas.

While much economic history has moved away from a focus on the stars and large-scale successes, this has been less the case in the analysis of business ideas and management philosophies. Studies of scientific management, for example, have traditionally ignored the breadth

DOI: 10.4324/9781003206996-4

of the work of Frederick Winslow Taylor and those who followed him who spelled out his philosophy more articulately. Instead, there has been considerable emphasis on his personal peculiarities or his earliest experiments. Moreover, as much focus has remained on Taylor's early work, that of his adherents has remained hidden. There are two issues here – first, Taylor's work has remained frozen a few efforts, despite the fact that like many scholars and practitioners, his work developed beyond his first (in)famous experiments. In many respects, Taylor regretted the infamy of these (Brown, 1954, 14). Second, the long-standing and rigid focus on aspects of Taylorism has marginalized or eliminated consideration of other elements of the movement which evolved from the First World War. The Bulletins of the Taylor Society attest to the evolution of scientific management and the richness therein.

The kinds of elision arguably evident in many analyses of social science investigations into scientific management emphasise the significance of scholarly investigation, and the centrality of applying a critical eye to unquestioned assumptions. They also illuminate patterns of transmission of ideas in scholarly disciplines. In cases such as this, the continuing uncritical acceptance of old 'truths' may have proved a barrier to scholarly progress and rigour. Investigating a modern unknown, especially one as prolific as Polakov, enables scholars to reconsider their unquestioned assumptions.

The paper is in three sections. In the first section, a brief discussion of scientific management delineates some of the differences in the conceptualisation of Taylorism or scientific management. There are evident differences between the views held by the movement's detractors and those held by the members of the Taylor Society. In the second section, the life and times of Polakov are briefly explored, focusing on his involvement in the Taylor Society, while in the third part the nature and extent of Polakov's socialism is surveyed and assessed in order to show that it was inextricably bound up in his scientific management.

Scientific management: definition and context[2]

A difficulty in much of the literature on scientific management is that analysts commonly begin with the assumption that the Taylorists held negative intent towards workers. This assumption then prefigures the investigation that will follow. Scientific management is thus frequently defined as depending on some form of time-and-motion study, by which management or employers strive to increase control over work through deskilling and degrading work. It is through such 'black-box' reductionism that the unquestioned assumptions of anti-unionist and relentless managerial exploitation are upheld (see e.g. Kanigel 1997, Nadworny, 1955). Even recent publications on the history of management have shown the limits of effectiveness of their scholarship when authors base their ideas on the *a priori* assumption that the system of scientific management

> . . . was based upon breaking a job down into its constituent elements. Unnecessary motions were dispensed with and each element was timed by means of a stop- watch.[3]

As the originator of scientific management, Frederick Winslow Taylor argued in the face of similar assertions, the traditional managerialist reasoning confuses the tools for the essence or philosophy.[4]

The narrow process of defining and 'examining' scientific management has been reversed in the last decade or so as Taylorism has been revisited by a number of scholars who have investigated scientific management unencumbered by these kinds of value-laden *a priori* assumptions.[5] Drawing most notably on the original material of the Taylorists in the Taylor Society,[6] these scholars have shown that the Taylorists can be marked off from what they called the cheap shams and 'stunt peddlers'. Moreover, close analysis of Taylor Society documents and the writings of Taylorists such as Morris Cooke and Harlow Person show how different the committed Taylorists were from those kinds of capitalists particularly favoured by the movement's detractors (and most modern textbook writers in business and social sciences). Many designated themselves scientific managers, but then invoked only a few 'shortcuts', rather than the whole method or philosophy. A commitment to the whole philosophy of scientific management is most clearly apparent in the Taylor Society, founded by those who knew Frederick Taylor and sought to emulate his philosophy and implement his ideas *in toto*. Taylor Society members reserved their strongest language for those who operated thus in the name of scientific management. The usually restrained Harlow Person, founding president and later managing director of the Taylor Society, for example, expressed the general view when he argued that:

> Just as there were fake physicians and shyster lawyers when medicine and law were young professions, so we have at present, fake organizing engineers. They do as much damage in the plants by which they are engaged as the fake physician did to the health of the patient. I wish it were possible . . . to abolish these fake and damaging self-styled organizing engineers.[7]

This is not to say that the definition of scientific management of the Taylor Society members was an absolute. The members of the Taylor Society were products of their time, when ideas of progress prevailed over static norms. Thus, while their normative assumptions did indeed cover a variety of perspectives, the scientific managers of the Taylor Society were generally activist or progressive social democrats,

> in an era dominated by widespread commitment to a passion for social progress . . . [and the need to] make politics more democratic, business more responsible and society more moral and more just.[8]

These ideas came under the banner of Progressivism, generally described as a 'pervasive but diffuse political movement' which was aimed against the corrupt big business and the politico-economic system which worked for the rich and against the poor. To remedy this, Schachter argues the Progressives typically promoted 'planned progress towards a better system'.[9] Just what these ideals meant and how to achieve them was a source of major debate in the first quarter of twentieth-century America and organisations such as the Taylor Society can be shown to contain as much intellectual ferment as in the wider society.[10]

Despite the shared commitment to scientific management as a holistic system, there was nevertheless a considerable array of perspectives. Where views differed among the scientific managers, these were on the level of emphasis as to which tools of measurement were most effective, and how scientific management could enhance economy and society. Their views on trade unions, for example, ranged from a belief that the development of an effective national trade union movement was essential to the view that shop committees were a more potent means of ensuring efficiency and fairness at the workplace.[11] There was also debate on how far Frederick Taylor's principles were inviolate. This was a particularly contentious area, because it brought the Society's commitment to critical analysis and progress into conflict with members' beliefs that what distinguished the 'real' Taylorists from the short-cut opportunists was unequivocal support of the principles of Frederick Taylor.[12] Perhaps the clearest example, though, of capacity of the 'true' scientific management to contain both Progressive and left-wing ideologies is to be found in the activities of Walter Polakov.

Walter Polakov: Taylorist

Walter Nicholas Polakov, a Russian immigrant, was educated in Moscow and then, around the turn of the century in Dresden, at the same time as Rosa Luxemburg was editing the SPD journal Sachsiche Arbeiterzeitung amidst the Revisionist controversy. Polakov's personal papers are so far untraceable, but given that he often quoted Luxemburg and like-minded fellow revolutionist, August Bebel, it seems possible that Polakov became aware of Luxemburg when he was an engineering student in Dresden. After Dresden, Polakov undertook further post-graduate study in industrial hygiene in Moscow and was possibly working at Tula Locomotive Works around the time of the 1905 Revolution. He arrived in the USA in 1906 with his wife and daughter, and set about learning English, a language over which he had considerable command within five years. He obtained work as an engineer with the American Locomotive Company, where he met Henry Laurence Gantt, whose devoted follower he remained for the rest of his life.[13]

Evidence that Polakov was a scientific manager is apparent in three ways. First, he was a full member of the Taylor Society from October 1915, joining in the same month as later luminaries in the Society, John Otterson and Keppele Hall.[14] To gain membership of the Taylor Society was a demanding process, with rigorous standards for qualification as a full member. These included both qualifications and experience, as signified by age – an applicant had to be at least 30 years old and to demonstrate involvement in, and commitment to, scientific management. Polakov's engineering degree from Dresden and his graduate study in Moscow prior to emigrating to the USA, together with his work with Gantt and as a consulting engineer, provided fitting qualifications for membership. As a respected power engineer (Wren, 1976a), Polakov worked primarily on increasing power plant efficiency at a time when there was a proliferation of small power stations for manufacturing plants, as well as the many privately owned power stations for domestic and commercial consumption. His commitment to science in industry included technological improvements, so that in years to come Polakov would be seen by some as 'an internationally known electrical engineer who had pioneered the development of remote control instrument boards'.[15]

Second, Polakov was an active participant in the Taylor Society until about 1921, and again in the 1930s after the Society merged with the Industrial Management Society. While membership records of Taylor Society are quite incomplete, there is a gap of about ten or so years from the early 1920s, when Polakov is not reported in debates and did not present any papers to the Society. He is certainly not in the list of members in 1929. This gap of ten years ties in with an apparent break between Polakov and executive members of the society around 1923 which appeared to centre around Polakov's belief that Henry L. Gantt was superior to Frederick Taylor.[16] While Polakov always paid homage to Taylor, his tribute was always muted or qualified by comparison with his views on Gantt.

It seems likely that Polakov was also personally devoted to Gantt. Polakov first came to Gantt's attention when the former was employed as an engineer at the American Locomotive Company. In 1910 he joined Gantt's consulting firm, although he left two years later to join the consulting firm of Charles Day, who was later to become Vice President of the Taylor Society. Remaining firm friends with both Gantt and Day, Polakov formed his own consulting business in 1915, and during the First World War he worked closely with Gantt coordinating ship production for the Emergency Fleet Corporation at a time when American ships were sustaining considerable damage in naval battles after the USA entered the war in 1917. As well, Gantt and Polakov, and other scientific managers such as Horace B. Drury, were employed to bring scientific management techniques to fleet deployment for the US Shipping Board.

The biographer, Alford, cites one of those who gave a eulogy at Gantt's funeral, and who remembered that Gantt indeed encouraged a group of younger men to become involved in his work. 'To work with Gantt was a great deal more than working for him, and in this relation he placed a confidence in his men which called for the best that could be given'.[17] That Gantt and Polakov were not only joint signatories in the breakaway group from American Society of Mechanical Engineers which called itself the New Machine, but that they also worked together on the numerous Navy projects attests to a close working relationship until Gantt's death in 1919.[18] Polakov's break with the Taylor Society in the early 1920s seems to have been a result of a disagreement between Polakov who wanted greater honours for Gantt, and the Taylor Society officers who gave primacy to Taylor.

Nevertheless, Polakov's commitment to, and conception of, scientific management was similar to other members of the Taylor Society. His definition of scientific management contained the same emphases on the scientific method, on thorough investigation, measurable outcomes and efficiency in effort and resources at plant level and beyond. He also had the same horror of what he called the 'stunt peddlers', and the same commitment to scientific management as a holistic practice.

What we mean here [by scientific management] . . . is of course not an agglomeration of short cuts, stunts and universal remedies for this and that industrial ills and waste, but an organically whole philosophy of industrial cooperation carried out for a common good.[19]

The third basis for identifying Polakov as having the same commitments to scientific management as those Taylorists noted above is found in the fact that Polakov was an earnest practising scientific manager who wrote extensively on scientific management, in general, and also specifically on power production.[20] He began publishing prolifically on scientific management from five years after immigrating to the USA, an impressive feat for someone who had arrived with little or no English. His first recorded publication in the USA was one of the early publications using the term 'scientific management', entitled 'Power Plant Betterment by Scientific Management' in *Engineering Magazine*.[21] It was in fact a series of articles totalling about sixty pages and dealing in great detail with methods of increasing productivity in electricity production through the implementation of scientific management. In these writings, as well his publications on aspects of fuel conservation and technocracy, Polakov's ideas were ground in his beliefs in both Marxism and scientific management. His first paper before the Taylor Society 'Planning Power Plant Work' is unreconstructed workplace Taylorism.[22] It uses twenty-seven charts and figures to describe production and work redesign in meticulous detail. While many of his later writings frequently took a broader focus, one of Polakov's central interests remained in the areas of industrial management based on scientific management principles. He made considerable use of Gantt charts and although outside the time frame of this paper, it is worth noting that much of his life's work was aimed at publicising the Gantt charts, including taking them to Russia in 1929–1931 where he was apparently the only American engineer working as a consultant on Stalin's first five-year plan.[23]

Although his ideological beliefs meant that Polakov always held a fairly wide and economic determinist view of society, the experience of the effectiveness of scientific management during the war heightened Polakov's awareness of the potential for scientific management well beyond the plant and workplace, as it did for most of the scientific managers. This is apparent in Polakov's writings, which prior to the First World War had been almost exclusively on aspects of workplace scientific management in power plants, albeit almost always with the expressed view that the capitalist employment relationship was essentially exploitative.

By 1922, he had published two books and about twenty scholarly articles on aspects of scientific management. In his writings, Polakov never ceased to emphasise the impact and importance of electricity as a technical and social benefit to society, but for him these benefits were greatly mitigated by the wastage that occurred as a consequence of sloppy production and the anarchic effects of the market. Both of these were anathema to Polakov, offending his vocation as a meticulous engineer and his ideology as a Marxist. While much of his writing centred on the methods and benefits of scientific management for power production, they were as much a vehicle for his economics and his political beliefs, as for his passions for scientific management and engineering. This is encapsulated in the first sentence of the Preface to his largest and arguably best work, a book of over 400 pages, entitled *Mastering Power Production.*

Efficiency in mastering the production of power received little attention under a regime aiming merely at the accumulation of profits rather than at rendering essential service for it was comparatively simple to transfer the cost of inefficiency and waste to the consumers through price increases.[24]

Polakov as a socialist scientific manager

Taylor Society debates were rich in innuendo and lively argument. It was in these discussions that Polakov offered his first recorded comments to the Society in December 1915. These are worth quoting more or less in full since they demonstrate the inextricability for Polakov of his commitments to socialism and to scientific management. In it Polakov was responding to Robert Valentine's paper on collective bargaining, 'The Progressive Relation between Efficiency and Consent':[25]

In his attempt to reconcile the methods of increasing productive efficiency with the consent of the workmen, Mr Valentine ignores the very basis of the economic form of our society. It is not the opinion of the individual workman or of workmen's societies, but of the class of wage earners, of the proletariat that we have to take into account. Modern society economically is composed of two classes, those who produce and those who give them the facilities to produce, of owners of physical energy to be sold for a living and owners of means of production such as natural resources, machinery and capital. The interests of these two classes of our society are diametrically opposed. Wage earners want to sell their labour at as a high a price as they can force the employer to give them. The employers want to sell the commodities produced by workmen for as high a price as they can get. Consumers as an economic class do not exist. They belong to both classes. Numerically however, the working class is not only to secure high wages as this automatically raises the price of commodities they produce, but also to reduce or at least stop the increased cost of commodities, that is, cost of living, which at present and in the past always increased in advance of and as a rule faster than the wages. The working class through their world-famous spokesmen scientifically analysed these aims of the working class and little, if anything remains to be said after the works of Carl (sic) Marx, Friedrich Engels, August Bebel and others were published.

To underline this last point, Polakov completed his contribution with a quote from *Women under Socialism*:

> The working class does welcome advance of science as applied to industries inasmuch as with increased speed of production made thereby possible, it is possible to reduce working hours to eight, six or even four per day, for education, for home life and for social activities. Here we have the consent to increase the productive efficiency and this consent comes not from casual association of individual workmen with demagogic politicians, but from the class conscious scientifically founded party that does represent the interests of the working class.[26]

These words and quotations of Polakov's are not stray ideas – Polakov repeated them in different forms and using different words for much of his life, though he sometimes masked the sources of his ideas to make them more palatable for his readers. Nor were Polakov's ideals merely rhetoric well removed from practice. At the same time as Polakov was quoting Bebel to the Taylor Society, he and Gantt were part of a breakaway group of ASME, known as the New Machine, which was a forerunner of the Technocrats of the 1930s. The New Machine aimed to give substance to the idea that engineers, who they believed were alone in understanding production, should take political action in order to achieve a better society. While it was partly Progressivist in its orientation, attacking as it did the financiers and bankers who controlled industry 'merely for profit', the New Machine included a number of engineers who became closely allied with the socialist group of Technocrats which made a meteoric appearance in the 1930s. The New Machine faded from existence after Gantt's death in 1919, but Polakov remained a technocrat and joined the ill-fated Technocratic movement after his return from Russia in 1931.[27]

Polakov's socialism is difficult to categorise. He was committed to the labour theory of value, and to the end of capitalism and rise of socialism as an inevitable outcome of the contradictions of capitalism, including the falling rate of profit. His books in particular demonstrated a thorough working knowledge of Marx's ideas, especially *Capital*, although he very rarely quoted *Capital* directly. Rather, he would convey Marx's ideas by citing American heroes like Benjamin Franklin or Abraham Lincoln, or the British idealist Tory Lord Leverhulme. At times, too, Polakov also promoted the concept of a cooperative commonwealth, and evolutionary socialism through government ownership especially of utilities. Stabile would argue these views reflected the right-wing socialism of early twentieth-century America, which had its source in the ideas of the revisionist Bernstein.[28]

The evidence is greater, however, that Polakov was not a revisionist but rather a strict Marxist who was more than usually cautious about proclaiming his beliefs, perhaps because he was a Russian immigrant. Certainly, some of those he knew perceived Polakov as a Marxist. Harold Loeb, an activist and analyst who had at one time had a close working relationship with Polakov, is reported as having stated in an interview in the 1950s that Polakov had read only one book in his life, Marx's *Capital*.[29] Polakov identified his debt as a scholar to Marxist analysis in his research and writings. All his major works began with historical analysis of the ideas and events which he was seeking to elucidate, and he continually emphasised the debt to generations before. As a necessary corollary, Polakov always gave credence to the labour theory of value. Thus,

> The foundation of our economic, industrial and business system lays in the service rendered by all the preceding generations. A sewing machine is capable of increasing the productivity of its operator, not only by the amount of labour worked into it by the mechanic but the integrated services of all the scientists philosophers, artisans etc. and of all those who directly served to make their life and work possible back from the ages of primitive man ... No man can today further develop the technique of production unless he is helped by this vast amount of knowledge which was accumulated in all countries and in all ages. . .[30]

These techniques of modern production have labour embodied in them, asserted Polakov, and the quantity of labour time is what gives the product, be it a pair of shoes or a kilowatt of electricity, its value. It is not because labour has a choice, but because 'we work to live'.

That work is essential in any society is, of itself, not a problem for Polakov, nor indeed was it for Marx, but two further points need to be made. The first is that under capitalism capital takes part of the value of labour for itself. As long as the means of production is privately owned and production is carried out for profit, rather than need or service, then the relations of production are unjust and class struggle is inevitable. Moreover, argues Polakov, what capital has done has been to encourage enormous wastage of human effort and natural resources. As long as profit and not production for the 'common weal' is the focus of economic activity, then capital will be uncaring of what is wasted.[31]

Given that differential pay rates were central to the scientific managers, it is useful to note how Polakov, the socialist scientific manager, deals with this issue. He does this by starting from the premise that the value of the commodities is contained in the labour provided by the worker. He then raises the question of whether the inequality of labour values through differential efficiency 'must fetch different labor-price (wages) and if so, whether this inequality of earnings endangers social equality and democratic principle'.[32] Following from Marx, Polakov has no problem with skill differentials, since for both of them different degrees of skill produce different values, and the value and therefore the wage of skilled or efficient labour is simply the value of the socially necessary labour-time required to produce a commodity multiplied by the level of skill or efficiency. Consideration of both skill and efficiency is well within the confines of the labour theory of value for Polakov, who draws on his distaste for wastefulness in justifying differential wages for the more efficient worker. Taking the example of an inefficient fireman shovelling coal into the furnace, in order to produce electricity, Polakov argues that not only is the labour-power of the inefficient worker worth less than that of his efficient work mate, but he also

> ... destroys the results of the work of miners who dug out the coal, of railroad men who that brought it in, of mechanics that built and repaired the machinery used in mining and transportation and scores of other men and women whose work was directly and indirectly needed to get to the boiler-room the coal which ... he sent up the chimney.[33]

The labour of the more efficient worker thus has greater value, of its own account, and on account of all the past labour-time. Consequently, 'different values of laboring power *must fetch different wages...*'. It is important to note here that Polakov was most scathing of terms like 'bonus plans', since for him they imply a gift or something that is given, rather than what is earned.

In responding to the question of equality from what Polakov calls the 'pseudo-democrats', he is similarly unequivocal, but here he calls his scientific management into play. He does this by arguing that not only is it true that 'the right of the producers [earnings] is proportional to the amount of work they furnish ...', but also that '*the equality con-sists in that the labour is measured by an equal standard*' (italics in original). Thus, argues Polakov, scientific management provides a method and a principle for the application of the labour theory of value.[34]

From the same traditions of analysis Polakov drew his belief in the inevitability of socialism, since the stage of capitalism would give way to 'a higher stage' which he argued was already revealing frailty, just as feudalism had given way to capitalism. This was evident, *inter alia*, in the tendency for the average rate of profit to fall, which, Polakov asserts, comes from the demands of competition. Such demands lead to a need to invest capital in better machinery and equipment, which in turn develops the tendency of the rate of profit to fall unless production is intensified and output of commodities grows. However, the necessity for higher investment develops a contradiction with the tendency: to limit the supply in order to maintain high prices and consequently, insists Polakov,

> such a policy causes a large proportion of expensive machinery to stay idle and accumulate burden, which being shifted on the shoulders of consumers in the form of price added to the goods manufactured with the balance of equipment works again toward the unbalancing the whole structure limiting the buying power of society.[35]

But, as Polakov notes, this means that the intensification of labour must be increased as a means of confronting the tendency of the average rate of profit to fall.[36]

However, while he sees the potential for scientific management as enhancing this intensification of labour, for Polakov this means reducing effort, and increasing the creativity and enjoyment of work.[37] Moreover, scientific management as Polakov portrays it is a necessary means of paving the way for socialism. It has the potential to do this in several ways. It focuses on production, rather than profit. It develops the practices of planning and recording efficient production for workers at all levels, and it provides a working environment and working conditions which are based on fairness through scientifically defined

goals jointly set with the workers. These attributes of scientific management become clearer if they are seen in the context of the inevitability of socialism. For in the new order of things to come,

> The principal thing to ascertain is the number of and the nature of
> the forces that are available, the quantity and the matter of the means
> of production. The next thing to ascertain is the quantity of supplies
> that are on hand. . . If for instance the demand is statistically estab-
> lished for bread, meat, shoes etc. and the productivity of the respec-
> tive plants is equally known, the average daily amount of socially
> necessary labour is thereby ascertained and . . . point out where more
> plants for the production of a certain article may be needed or where
> such may be discontinued . . . or turned to other purpose.[38]

For Polakov, who saw scientific management as fulfilling these requirements, the new order was imminent. Not only had the Bolshevik
revolution occurred, an event he is generally careful to couch in the
most general terms, but also in the USA the need during the war to or-
ganise production for the sake of national need, rather than profit, was
a self-evident lesson in the worth of the national need as the basis for
production. However, even if the new economic order was not immediately near at hand, Polakov believed that scientific management, as
practised properly, and not by charlatans and 'stunt peddlers', was an
inevitable and necessary set of principles in order to ensure efficiency
and improvement of both production and the working environment.

> The economic evolution of society goes in a definite direction and
> it is not within anyone's power to divert or retard its progress. All
> that can be done is to choose the means to reduce the pains and
> sufferings caused by the transition period.[39]

It is important to note that as well as a scientific manager and Marxist,
there is no doubt that Polakov was also unrelentingly an engineer. His
journal articles and books up to 1922, and indeed beyond, are those
of one who is trained and committed to making the machines work
better. He goes into immense detail about engineering matters in all
of his publications, and as noted previously, in some circles his fame
rested on his role as a significant developer of instrument control systems. He was also undoubtedly a Technocrat, who believed that the
engineers, above any other profession, could superintend the social,
economic and physical aspects of production, and not only at plant
level. All of his ideals, as engineer, scientific manager and Marxist,

are focused on waste. Polakov abhorred waste, whether it be wasted human effort, wasted natural resources or unnecessary labour, in the form of advertising agents and salespersons. To his mind this dissipation had its foundation in capitalism and competition for profit, albeit sometimes couched quite cautiously, just as his references to Marx are nearly always concealed.

Despite his caution, Polakov never concealed his Marxism within the Taylor Society debates, and even in his writings though he uses sources that might have been more palatable to his reader, his debt and commitment to Karl Marx are apparent to those with any familiarity with Marx's writing. What makes Polakov's open expressions of his beliefs in his books and in his recorded comments at Taylor Society meetings up to 1921 more piquant was that these were said or written at a time when the 'red scares' were at a peak, and a young J. Edgar Hoover was developing his skills. For example, Polakov was writing his book *Mastering Power Production* at the time of the famous night of January 2, 1920 when 10,000 people were arrested for being 'liberal' or socialist or Bolshevik, and when a common tactic was to 'redball' every 'liberal' who believed in municipal or government ownership.[40] At the same time the Federal Commissioner of Education was speaking for many in high places when he was reported as saying that

> there was altogether too much preaching these damnable doctrines of Bolshevism, anarchy, communism, and socialism, . . . if I had my way, I would not only imprison but would expatriate all advocates of these dangerous un-American doctrines. I would even execute every one of them – and do it joyfully.[41]

Ignoring the difficulties inherent in simultaneously imprisoning, expatriating and executing such perpetrators, the sentiments expressed in such views were widely disseminated through the newspapers. The history of the USA, especially after the Bolshevik revolution, is replete with examples of the concerted and extensive efforts to rid the nation of socialism. That Polakov proclaimed these damnable doctrines in Taylor Society meetings quoting Marx, Bebel or Luxemburg is not only further evidence of the breadth of views apparent in the Taylor Society, but also evidence of the ways in which true scientific management was eminently compatible with ideologies beyond the predominantly social democratic Progressivism.

Polakov's caution in his written work, which can give the appearance that he may have been an evolutionary socialist, was perhaps determined by the very predominance of these views. As a migrant, a resident of New

York, and a Russian, he was undoubtedly aware of the very famous 'expatriation' of Emma Goldman. And he was undoubtedly faced with this possibility if he did not stay within the bounds of acceptability. On the other hand, this may well have been because, rather than a fear of expatriation, he felt he could be more effective as a practitioner-intellectual. As Luxemburg's biographer, Nettl, has argued, when analysing the dissonance between practice and preaching of Rosa Luxemburg in her responses to Lenin around the turn of the century,

> The difficult relationship between ideology and pragmatic action has been identified as a continuing problem for all political parties, irrespective of their ideology – but the more intense the ideology the greater the difficulty. Where does the relevance of ideological assertions for practical politics end, and mere functional symbolism or ritual for purposes of ensuring unity or legitimacy begin?[42]

The Russian immigrant who was publishing widely and who had found his place within the societies of managers and engineers may well also have decided that the forum closer to the centre was more effective than to be at the margin.

Conclusion

At least during the second and third decades of the twentieth century, the Taylor Society was an organisation for those who believed in a philosophy and practice of management founded on the scientific method, as inherited from Frederick Winslow Taylor. Inherent in the 'pure' Taylorist philosophy were teamwork, planning and a production focus that saw industry as dynamic, rather than static. Although the Taylorists were mainly of social democratic or Progressivist persuasions, none of these foci of themselves required a particular ideological stance. As any reading of the debates of the Taylor Society reveal,

> the Society was avowedly plural in its membership and in the openness of its debates, even to the extent that socialist idealism could be expressed and recorded in the journal of the Society at a time when media and governments were attempting to outlaw such idealism in any way possible. This is apparent in the place of Walter Polakov, a Marxist and dedicated scientific manager.

In the Taylor Society, he was not a significant personage in that he never held office, and indeed gave up his membership for over a decade. Nevertheless, he was a registered member and participant until the early 1920s, and his writings always promoted the significance and worth of scientific management from a socialist perspective. Polakov was not a great luminary like Morris Cooke, for example, yet his research and accounts of practice were of sufficient standard to be published in major engineering journals. Moreover, to understand a philosophical movement or, indeed, an academic discipline, it is important not only to examine the work of the 'stars', but also those who are the foot-soldiers, the less stellar, but core scholars. This is particularly important in the history of business ideas, where there are multiple and often competing perspectives. An important role of the historian is to explicate and amplify the voices less heard, for then we are practising rigorous scholarship to which we all aspire.

Given the evidence in this paper through the analysis of the life and work of Walter Polakov, continuing re-evaluation of Taylorism seems to be justified.

Notes

1 Rather than the purist Lockean sense the term 'liberals' is used here in the American sense of giving higher priority to issues such as social justice, equity and fairness, than those who would presume that the wants of business and the market are paramount.

2 This section is an abbreviated discussion of a much more extensive analysis of Taylor Society debates.

3 C. Wright, *The Management of Labour* (Melbourne, Oxford University Press, 1995) p. 26; see also D. Stabile, *Prophets of Order*, Boston, Southend Press, 1964) and D. Collins, *Organizational Change: Sociological Perspectives* (London, Routledge, 1998), for the fragmented view of scientific management from the broader social sciences. Historians such as Kanigel, 1997 and Merkle, 1980 provide lengthy scholarly discussions, yet still failed to move beyond the time-and-motion interpretation.

4 It is curious that attacks on Taylorism or scientific management frequently draw upon the doubtless eccentricities of F. W. Taylor, beginning with his problematic experiment with 'the dumb ox worker Schmidt', yet recollections of the personal habits of other management innovators from Mayo to Deming rarely, if ever, feature in analysis of their philosophies or experiments.

5 See especially D. Nelson, 'Scientific management and the workplace, 1920–1935' in Jacoby, S. M. (ed.) *Masters to Managers: Historical and Comparative Perspectives on American Employers* (New York, Columbia University Press, 1992); C. T. Nyland, *Reduced Worktime and the Management of Production* (New York, Cambridge University Press, 1989); Nyland, C. (1995) 'Taylorism and hours of work', *Journal of Management History*, 1(2), pp. 8–26; Nyland, C. (1995) 'Taylorism, John R. Commons, and the Hoxie report', *Journal of Economic Issues*, 30(4) pp. 985–1017.

112   *Diana Kelly*

E. Tsunoda, 'Rationalizing Japan's political economy: The business initiative, 1920–1955' (Unpublished PhD Thesis, Graduate School of Arts and
Sciences, Columbia University; 1993); H. L. Schachter, *Frederick Taylor
and the Public Administration Community: A Reevaluation* (Albany, State
University Press of New York, 1989).

6 Originally called Society to Promote the Science of Management. In the
1930s after mergers it was called the Society for the Advancement of Management (S.A.M.), which is still active.

7 H. S. Person, 'Scientific management', *Bulletin of the Taylor Society*, 2, 3
October, 1916, p. 21; see also H. S. Person, 'The manager, the workman
and the social scientist: their functional interdependence as observers and
judges of industrial mechanisms', *Bulletin of the Taylor Society*, 3(1), 1917,
pp. 1–7. (hereafter *BTS*).

8 R. H. Hofstadter, W. Miller and D. Aaron, *The American Republic, Volume Two Since 1865* (New Jersey, Prentice-Hall, 1959), pp. 354–360.

9 Schachter 'Frederick Taylor', p. 51ff.

10 See *Bulletin of the Taylor Society (BTS)*, the journal of the Society which presented not only papers of members and invited speakers, but also transcripts
of parts of the debates which followed presentations. See e.g. Discussion, of
R. G. Valentine's paper 'The progressive relationship between efficiency and
consent', *Bulletin of The Taylor Society*, 2(1), January, 1916, pp. 13–20.

11 See *BTS*, 1916–1919, especially Discussion following Cooke's paper, 'Cen-
tralization of Administrative Authority; Cooke, M. L., S. Gompers and
F. Miller (eds) (1920) 'Labor, management and production', *The Annals*,
v. XCI, September; see also Person 'manager workman'; pp. 1–3; F. W.
Taylor, 'Scientific management and labor unions', *Bulletin of the Society
to Promote the Science of Management*, 1(1), December, 1914, p. 3; R. G.
Valentine, 'The progressive relationship', pp. 11–13 and records of 'Discussions' of these papers in *BTS*.

12 Schachter notes that Taylor bluntly refused to join the Efficiency Society
because he claimed it was full of shortcut merchants.

13 The sources for this section D. A. Wren, 'From the management of produc-
tion to the management of society', *The Conference Board Record*, XIII(6),
1976a, pp. 40–42; D. A. Wren, 'Scientific management in the USSR, with
particular reference to the contribution of Walter N. Polakov', *Academy of
Management Review*, 5, January, 1976b, pp. 1–11; H. Elsner, *The Technocrats:
Prophets of Automation*, Syracuse, Syracuse University Press, 1967; W. N.
Polakov, 'Power Plant Betterment by Scientific Management', *Engineering
Magazine* (NY), 41, 1912, pp. 101–112, 278–292, 448–456, 577–582, 798–809,
970–975; W. N. Polakov, *Man and His Affairs from an Engineering Point of
View*, Baltimore, Williams, 1921a; W. N. Polakov, 'Making work fascinat-
ing', *ASME Journal*, December; 1921b; W. N. *Mastering Power Production:
The Industrial, Economic and Social Problems Involved and Their Solution*,
London, Cecil Palmer, 1922 (MPP); W. N. Polakov, 'The Gantt Chart in
Russia', *American Machinist*, 75, 1931, pp. 261–264; W. N. Polakov, 'Discus-
sion of Robert Valentine, 'The progressive relations between efficiency and
consent', *BTS*, November, 1916, pp. 16–17; W. N. Polakov, *The Power Age:
Its Quest and Challenge*, New York, Covici Friede Publishers, 1933.

14 *Bulletin of Society to Promote the Science of Management*, Vol. 1, 6, 1915, p. 1.

15 Elsner, *Technocrats*, p. 60.

16 Communication, H. Person to Cooke; Morris Cooke Papers – Correspondence.
17 W. E. Pulis, cited in L. P. Alford, *Henry Laurence Gantt: Leader in Industry*, American NY, Society of Mechanical Engineers, 1934, p. 242.
18 Alford, in *Gantt*, 1934, pp. 251–299; See also Wren, 'From management of production', p. 41
19 Polakov, *MPP*, p. 42.
20 The bibliography only cites a very few of Polakov's writings, mainly 1911–1922. Polakov was writing until well into the 1940s, when he was Engineering Director of United Mineworkers of America.
21 Polakov, 'Power plant betterment'.
22 Polakov, 'Planning', pp. 1–23.
23 Polakov, *Power Age*; Polakov, 'The Gantt chart'; the Gantt charts remained central to Soviet economic development. See also Wren, 'Scientific management, Russia'.
24 Polakov, *MPP*, p. ix.
25 Valentine, 'The progressive relationship', pp. 11–13.
26 Bebel, cited by Polakov in Discussion, of R. G. Valentine's paper, pp. 16–17.
27 Polakov's links with technocracy are also evident from a long acquaintanceship with Howard Scott, the leading technocrat. It was apparent from Polakov's contribution to the discussion of Hugh Archbald's presentation on mine management at the December 1919 Taylor Society meeting that he and Scott had discussed their respective comments prior to the meeting. It was perhaps no coincidence that Scott and Polakov attended this meeting together. Both of them had deeply admired Gantt who had died quite unexpectedly less than a month previously. Polakov also had links with the technocrat, Walter Rautenstrauch, of Columbia University.
28 Stabile, *Prophets of Order*.
29 Elsner, *Technocrats*.
30 Polakov, *MPP*, pp. 173–174.
31 Polakov, *Man and His Affairs*; Polakov, 'Making work fascinating'.
32 Polakov, *MPP*, p. 212.
33 Polakov, *MPP*, p. 212; Compare for example with K. Marx (1954) *Capital*, Volume I, London Lawrence A Wishart, 1954, pp. 567–569.
34 Polakov, *MPP*, pp. 211–213.
35 Polakov, *MPP*, pp. 9–11.
36 K. Marx, *Capital*, Volume III, Moscow, Progress Publishers, 1959, pp. 211–231.
37 Polakov, *Man and His Affairs*; Polakov, *MPP*.
38 Bebel, cited in Polakov, *MPP*.
39 Polakov, *MPP*, p. 12.
40 P. C. Sexton, *The War on Labor and the Left: Understanding America's Unique Conservatism*, Boulder, Westview Press, 1991, p. 134; See also P. S. Foner, *The Bolshevik Revolution: Its Impact on American Radicals, Liberals, and Labor: A Documentary Study*, New York, International Publishers, 1967.
41 Sexton, *The War*, p. 135.
42 J. P. Nettl, *Rosa Luxemburg*, Oxford, Oxford University Press, (abridged edition) 1969, p. 197.

114   *Diana Kelly*

Bibliography

Alford, L. P. (1934) *Henry Laurence Gantt: Leader in Industry*, American Society of Mechanical Engineers, New York.

Brown, J. A. C. (1954) *The Social Psychology of Industry: Human Relations in the Factory*, Harmondsworth, Penguin.

Bulletin of the Society to Promote the Science of Management, 1914–1915.

Bulletin of the Taylor Society 1916–1919 (*BTS*).

Cohen, G. A. (1988) *History, Labour and Freedom: Themes from Marx*, Clarendon Press, Oxford.

Collins, D. (1998) *Organizational Change: Sociological Perspectives*, Routledge, London.

Cooke, M. L., S. Gompers and F. Miller (eds) (1920) 'Labor, Management and Production', *The Annals*, v. XCI, September.

Drury, H. B. (1916) 'Scientific Management and Progress', *BTS*, 2, 4 November, pp. 1–10.

Discussion, of R. G. (1916) Valentine's paper 'The Progressive Relationship Between Efficiency and Consent', *Bulletin of the Taylor Society*, 2(1), January, pp. 13–20.

Elsner, H. Jr (1967) *The Technocrats: Prophets of Automation*. Syracuse University Press, Syracuse.

Foner, P. S. (1967) *The Bolshevik Revolution: Its Impact on American Radicals, Liberals, and Labor: a Documentary Study*, International Publishers, New York.

Hofstadter, R. H., Miller, W. and Aaron, D. (1959) *The American Republic, Volume Two Since 1865*, Prentice-Hall, New Jersey.

Hoxie, R. (1915) *Scientific Management and Labor*, Appleton, New York (reprint, Augustus M. Kelley, 1966).

Kanigel, R. (1997) *The One Best Way. Frederick Winslow Taylor and the Enigma of Efficiency*, Viking, New York.

Marx, K. (1954) *Capital*, Volume I, Lawrence A. Wishart, London Marx, K. (1959) *Capital*, Volume III, Progress Publishers, Moscow.

Merkle, J. A. (1980) *Management and Ideology: The Legacy of the International Scientific Management Movement*, University of California Press, Berkeley.

Nadworny, M. (1955) *Scientific Management and the Unions 1900–1932: A Historical Analysis*, Harvard University Press, Cambridge, MA.

Nelson, D. (1992a) *A Mental Revolution: Scientific Management since Taylor*, Ohio State University Press, Columbus.

Nelson, D. (1992b) 'Scientific Management and the Workplace, 1920–1935', in Jacoby, S. M. (ed.) *Masters to Managers: Historical and Comparative Perspectives on American Employers*, Columbia University Press, New York, pp. 74–89.

Nettl, J. P. (1969) *Rosa Luxemburg*, Oxford University Press, Oxford (abridged edition).

Nyland, C. (1989) *Reduced Worktime and the Management of Production*, Cambridge University Press, Melbourne.

Nyland, C. (1995a) 'Taylorism and Hours of Work', *Journal of Management History*, 1(2), pp. 8–26.

Nyland, C. (1995b) 'Taylorism, John R. Commons, and the Hoxie Report', *Journal of Economic Issues*, 30(4), pp. 985–1017.

Person, H. S. (1916) 'Scientific Management', *Bulletin of the Taylor Society*, 2, 3 October, pp. 16–23.

Person, H. S. (1917) 'The Manager, the Workman and the Social Scientist: Their Functional Interdependence as Observers and Judges of Industrial Mechanisms', *Bulletin of the Taylor Society*, 3(1), pp. 1–7.

Platt, J. (1996) *A History of Sociological Research Methods in America, 1920–1960*, Cambridge University Press, New York.

Polakov, W. N. (1912) 'Power Plant Betterment by Scientific Management', *Engineering Magazine* (NY), 41, pp. 101–112, 278–292, 448–456, 577–582, 798–809, 970–975.

Polakov, W. N. (1916) 'Discussion of Robert Valentine, "The Progressive Relations Between Efficiency and Consent"', *Bulletin of Taylor Society*, November, pp. 7–17.

Polakov, W. N. (1921a) *Man and His Affairs from an Engineering Point of View*, Williams, Baltimore.

Polakov, W. N. (1921b) 'Making Work Fascinating' *ASME Journal*, December.

Polakov, W. N. (1922) *Mastering Power Production: The Industrial, Economic and Social Problems Involved and Their Solution*, Cecil Palmer, London.

Polakov, W. N. (1931) 'The Gantt Chart in Russia', *American Machinist*, 75, pp. 261–264.

Polakov, W. N. (1933) *The Power Age: Its Quest and Challenge,* Covici Friede Publishers, New York.

Schachter, H. L. (1989) *Frederick Taylor and the Public Administration Community: A Reevaluation*, State University Press of New York, Albany.

Schachter, H. L. (2002) 'Women, Progressive-Era Reform, and Scientific Management', *Administration and Society*, 34(5) pp. 563–579.

Sexton, P. C. (1991) *The War on Labor and the Left: Understanding America's Unique Conservatism*, Westview Press, Boulder.

Stabile, D. (1964) *Prophets of Order*, Southend Press, Boston.

Taylor, F. W. (1914) 'Scientific Management and Labor Unions', *Bulletin of the Society to Promote the Science of Management*, I(I), December, p. 3.

Tsunoda, E. (1993) 'Rationalizing Japan's Political Economy: The Business Initiative, 1920–1955' Unpublished PhD Thesis, Graduate School of Arts and Sciences, Columbia University.

Valentine, R, G. (1916) 'The Progressive Relationship Between Efficiency and Consent', *Bulletin of the Taylor Society*, 2(1), January, pp. 7–13.

Whiteley, A. (1995) *Managing Change: A Core Values Approach*, Macmillan, South Melbourne.

Wren, D. A. (1976a) 'From the Management of Production to the Management of Society', *The Conference Board Record*, XIII(6), pp. 40–42.

Wren, D. A. (1976b) 'Scientific Management in the USSR, with Particular Reference to the Contribution of Walter N. Polakov', *Academy of Management Review*, 5, January, pp. 1–11.

Wren, D. A. (1987) *The Evolution of Management Thought*, (3rd edn), John Wiley and Son, New York.

Wright, C. (1995) *The Management of Labour*, Oxford University Press, Melbourne.

Retrospective

Marxist manager amidst the Progressives: Walter N. Polakov and the Taylor Society

Diana Kelly

It is said that everyone has 20–20 vision with hindsight. Certainly, there is much I can 'see' now, that I could not 'see' or know in 2002 when I wrote this piece. In part, that reflects the much greater information accessible now, than was available around the turn of this century, the mushrooming of available internet sources having been a boon for historians. In other cases, however, my imagination was greater than my evidence. For example, Polakov did not arrive in the USA in 1906 with his daughter as I stated (Kelly, 2003, p. 64). Rather, Polakov adopted Catherine several years later in 1910, around the same time his wife Antoinette left him. A minor detail which does not interfere with the objectives of the story but good history should be as accurate as possible.

There are other gaps – I made no mention of his work as a unionist fighting for mine safety and health care for miners with the UMWA. Nor was there mention of the FBI surveillance of Polakov, including FBI agents interviewing almost everyone in his local area, such that he eventually fled from Virginia to California (Kelly, 2016a). Such material would have substantiated the claims for the complexity and pro-worker potential evident in scientific management ideals (Kelly, 2016b). In the meantime, the digitisation of FBI records, and the impressive ways in which historians of ideas have used them have been notable developments.

I also treated the notions of Progressivism and Marxism as unchallenged terms for homogenous concepts, although both are deeply contested. But, for example, it is important to note that in his writings, Polakov's Marxism was seemingly of the Second International variety, more acceptably 'scientific' and aligned with modernist ideals in mainstream USA. These contrasted with the radical and militant kind of Marxism associated with his hero Rosa Luxemburg, who asserted mass activity as the revolutionary core of Marxism.

Another of my main criticisms when I first re-read this piece was about writing style. In particular, I was unimpressed with my tendency to be prolix and sesquipedalian. Oh those long words and wordy sentences! Fifteen years in a history department has surely given me a better appreciation of conciseness. My belated apologies to the then *JIH* editor, John Wilson, who raised questions about verbosity but forbore from taking a very red pencil to the prose.

In part, I think John's kindly collegiality came from his awareness and empathy that I had found precious few outlets to publish Polakov's story. Management scholars and editors resisted any topic that was too close to socialism, and socialist intellectuals were repelled by any positive mention of scientific management. For both groups, what I was proposing was such an anathema to their foundation assumptions; it was inconceivable that socialist and scientific management ideologies could be integrated in any way. Scholarly practices have moved on since 2003, but that resistance still abounds, especially outside management and labour history. Scholars in cognate disciplines are not expected to do new research outside their field, so they consult older texts which still purvey the earlier 'tram track' ideas. For example, in my recent book on Polakov (Kelly, 2020), I showed how historian Mike Wallace in his generally grand, modern history of New York, *Greater Gotham*, casually inserted the narrow, rigid and exploitative view of scientific management, as if it were an uncontested fact (Wallace, 2017). The urban historian can only depend on what he reads, and this unilateral view was what he found.

These processes highlight how the transmission of ideas in inexact fields like history and other social sciences and humanities can be directed or elided. Perspectives and perceptions can become either the metropole or the margin, depending on authors of influence, and standard understandings in a field. Like the 'shortcut merchants' so despised by the Taylor Society of 1910s and 1920s, so too researchers had neat boxes for their ideas, not to be looked into or rearranged for fear of changing what they knew to be 'truths' (Kelly, 2016a). The question then becomes, how can we now change the behemoth of timeworn simplistic ideas, such that scholars outside our field will no longer casually accept the old ossified beliefs?

Finally, it is important to note that in 2003, *JIH* gave me an opportunity to publish some aspects of the life of Walter Polakov, as a means of contributing to the burgeoning revisionist literature developed by others (see e.g. Bruce and Nyland, 2001; Nyland, Bruce and Burns, 2014; Schachter, 2018). It was not the first time aspects of Polakov's life, ideals and ideology had been published in academic press – that honour goes to Daniel Wren (Wren, 1980). However, 2003 piece showed, in a new way, that simplistic interpretations of scientific management should be treated with caution. In this respect, I rather enjoyed re-reading the last two sentences of the article:

> An important role of the historian is to explicate and amplify the voices less heard, for then we are practising [the] rigorous

scholarship to which we all aspire. Given the evidence in this paper through the analysis of the life and work of Walter Polakov, continuing re-evaluation of Taylorism seems to be justified.

(Kelly, 2003)

For these reasons, I would still recommend this piece.

Finally, it is worth noting that this project has been of the increasingly rare sort of research – *long research* – which takes decades to research and develop. Today, the pressures on academics emphasise short-term outcomes and multiple publications. The history and deep research into forgotten lives, such as those of Polakov, seem to have less and less value to the modern neoliberal university.

Wollongong
January 2021

References

Bruce, K. and Nyland, C. 2001 Scientific management and institutionalism and business stabilization: 1903–1923, *Journal of Economic Issues*, 35, 4, pp. 955–978.

Bruce, K. and Nyland, C. 2012 Democracy or Seduction? The Demonization of Scientific Management and the Deification of Human Relations, in Lichtenstein, N. and Shermer, E. (eds), *The American Right and labor: Politics, Ideology, and Imagination*, (pp. 42–76). University of Pennsylvania Press, Philadelphia.

Kelly, D. 2003 Marxist Manager Amidst the Progressives: Walter N. Polakov and the Taylor Society, *Journal of Industrial History*, 6, 2, pp. 61–75.

Kelly, D. 2016a The Scientific Manager and the FBI: The Surveillance of Walter Polakov in the 1940s, *American Communist History*, 15, 1, pp. 35–57.

Kelly, D. 2016b Perceptions of Taylorism and a Marxist Scientific Manager, *Journal of Management History*, 22, 3, pp. 298–319.

Kelly, D. 2020 *The Red Taylorist: The Life and Times of Walter Nicholas Polakov*, Emerald Publishing, Bingley, UK.

Nyland, C., Bruce, K. and Burns, P. 2014 Taylorism, the International Labour Organization, and the Genesis and Diffusion of Codetermination, *Organization Studies*, 35, 8, pp. 1149–1169.

Schachter, H. L. 2018 Labor at the Taylor Society: Scientific Management and a Proactive Approach to Increase Diversity for Effective Problem Solving, *Journal of Management History*, 24, 1, pp. 7–19.

Wallace, M. 2017 *Greater Gotham: A history of New York City from 1898 to 1919*. Oxford University Press, New York.

Wren, D. A. 1980 Scientific Management in the U.S.S.R. With Particular Reference to the Contribution of Walter N. Polakov, *Academy of Management Review*, 5, 1, pp. 1–11.

Index

Note: **Bold** page numbers refer to tables; *italic* page numbers refer to figures and page numbers followed by "n" denote endnotes.

Academic Approach 5, 11–14, 29–31
Accenture 87
Alexander Hamilton Church 17, 52, 91n6
Anne Shaw Organisation 16, 38n85
Associated Industrial Consultants (AIC) 23–24, 78–79, 93n30; central training 24; general training 24; site training 24
Attwood, Wallace 17

Baillieu Committee, formation of 8
Bebel, August 100, 104, 109
Bedaux approach 71–73, 92n14, 93n24
'Bedaux Engineers' 21, 73
'Bedaux Representatives' 19
Bedford Work-Study School 24, 76–77, 78
Berle, A. A. 3, 42
'Big Four' 16, 35n48, 77–78, 82, 93n30
Bolshevik revolution 108–109
Bonaparte, Napoleon 57
Boston Consulting Group's London programme 88
British Commercial Gas Association (BCGA) 16
British Computer Society's Certificate in IS Consultancy Practice 89
British Institute of Management (BIM) 5, 9–10

British management consultancy: corporate consultant strength 69; cost accounting 68; evolution of training 69; factors dominating consultancy 68–69; formal training for consultants 66; lack of expertise of consulting engineers 66, 68; management consulting service, 1869 68; of nineteenth century 68; phases of education and training (*see* education and training, phases of); production efficiency 68; 'quiet periods' 68
Burnham, J. 2, 40, 41, 47

'Centre for Management Studies' 9
Certificate and Diploma in Management Studies 8, 31, 33n15
Certificate in IS Consultancy Practice 89
Certified Management Consultant (CMC) qualification 88–89
Chandler, A. D. 3, 41, 42, 43, 44, 50, 51, 56
Charles Day 101
Charles E. Bedaux and Company 15, 70, 71, 72
'A Conspectus of Management Education' 9, 94n40
'The Conspectus' series 10–11, 33n20
consultancy approach 2; Academic Approach 29–31; contribution

made by consultants 30; Corporate Approach 31; Handy's three approaches 28; management consultants 32; 'Management Movement' 30; method of training delivery 30, 32; Professional Approach 29–31; Training Within Industry scheme 31; 'Urwick Report' 30

consultants, input of: 'The Administration of Marketing and Selling' 19; adoption of management modules 18; Associated Industrial Consultants (AIC) 23–24; Bedaux company, formation of 15, 19; 'Bedaux Representatives' 19; 'Big Four' 16; consultancy services 16; co-operation with Industrial League and Council 18–19; creation of training centres 23; direct and indirect educational inputs **26,** 26–27; direct role 15, 17; disadvantages 22–23; early consultancy in Britain 17; Federation of British Industries (FBI) 25; formation of Work-Study School at Bedford 25; functional methods and techniques 27; Henley Management Centre 25; indirect role 15, 17; involvement of management consultants 17; Management Consultancies Association (MCA) 26, 27, 28; management consultant companies and sole practitioners 16–17; management education and training, 1970s and 1980s 14; management information processes 15; models of management education and training, 1980s 14; PA Consulting Group 16; Personnel Administration 21; 'Process Analysis Method of Training' 21–22; Production Engineering (P-E) 24; production for 'luxury goods' 20; productivity levels 21; professional approach 20; 'Skills Analysis Training' 22; Slough Training Centre 24, 25;

specialist subjects 27; 'Stocktaking on Management Education' 25–26; 'Student Weeks of Management Training' 27–28; Sundridge Park 25; Urwick Management Centre 25
Cooke, M. L. 98, 111
Corporate Approach 5, 11, 12, 13, 31

Dahrendorf, R. 41, 42
The Decline of the British Economy (Elbaum and Lazonick) 49
'Department of Business Studies' 9
'Department of Industrial Administration' 9
digital learning strategies, employment of 87
Discipline and Punish (Foucault) 53
Drury, Horace B. 101

Eastman Kodak Company 70
Education Act, 1944 7
education and training, phases of 67; beginnings of off-site training (off-site training phase, 1941–1960s) 3, 76–79; current, mixed phase (1990s–present) 85–89, 90–91; expansion and specialisation (specialisation phase, 1960s–1990s) 80–85; first consultant training (on-the-job training phase, 1926–1941) 3, 70–76; pre-education and training phase (1869–1925) 89–90
e-education strategies 86–87
Elbaum, B. 49
Elbourne, E. T. 31
Engels, Friedrich 104

Factory Administration and Accounts in 1914 (Elbourne) 18
Federation of British Industries (FBI) 25
Ferguson, Michael 2, 3
'field engineers' 92n9
Foucault, Michel 3, 40, 60, 61; 'the disciplines' 53–54, 55, 56, 58; 'general method' 56, 57; 'great uniform machinery of prison' 53–54; 'History of Detail' 57; history of prison 53; lack of intentionality 56; nature of

social transformations 56; power, techniques of 56, 57–58; trained obedience 54–55
Foundation for Management Education 33n19
Franklin, Benjamin 105
full employment, concept of 7

Gantt, Henry L. 100, 101, 102

Handy, C. 5, 11, 25, 28, 31
Henley Management Centre 25
Herbert Austin 59
Hoover, J. Edgar 109
Hoskin, K. W. 52

ICI 59
Industrial Administration 9, 18
Industrial Management (Bedaux) 71
"industrial revolution" 45, 61n9
information technology: development of 95n43; effects of 85
Institute of Industrial Administration 18, 31
Institute of Management Consultants (IMC) 84, 95n44
institutional change: agenda of pre-nationalisation management 60; boards of directors 48; 'descending analysis' 50; development of US 'science of organisation' 51; domination of managerial corporations 58; geo-political model 47; internalising of transactions 50–51; invention of new organisational structures and control techniques 60–61; level of co-ordination 49; management accounting techniques 52–53; management capacity 60; managerial capacity 51; and managerial revolution, UK business 58–61; market-expansion driven 50; nationalisation, anti-trust and Industrial Reorganisation Corporation 59; nature of essential elements 58–59; non-technological organisational and management accounting inventions 51–52; scientific management

and management accounting 59; separation of ownership and control 48, 49, 53; and societal change (*see* Foucault, Michel); surplus management capacity 52; theory of 'Personal Capitalism' 49
International Council of Management Consulting Institutes (ICMCI) 95n49
Internet, introduction and use of 85, 87

Journal of Industrial History (JIH) 1–2, 4

Kelly, D. 3

Lazonick, W. 49
Lever Brothers 59
Leverhulme, Tory Lord 105
Lincoln, Abraham 105
Locke, R. R. 51
Loeb, Harold 105
Luxemburg, Rosa 100, 109, 110, 116

Macve, R. H. 52
Management Consultancies Association (MCA) 26, 27, 28, 38n85
management education and training, models of: 'Academic Approach' 5; 'after-work study' 6; in Britain 11; career development 6; concept of full employment 7; 'A Conspectus of Management Education' 9; 'The Conspectus' series 10–11; consultancy approach 2, 5, 6, 28–32; 'Corporate Approach' 5; Council for Academic Awards 10; development of 6; 'Direct' and 'Indirect' roles 6; educational platform for managers 8; employability and knowledge 7; Foundation for Management Education in 1960, formation of 9; input of consultants 14–28; making of managers 5, 6, 11–14; new Labour Government 7; 'Professional Approach' 5; in twentieth century to 1980s 6–11

'Management Movement' 30
Managerial Revolution (Burnham) 47
managerial revolution, Britain
    2–3; Big Government and Big
    Corporation 46–47; combination
    of large size, central strategic
    control and flexibility 45;
    competitive impact of US
    corporate practice 44; constant
    innovation 45; corporate
    responsibility and social consensus
    42; divorce of ownership and
    control 41–42; emergence of
    'modern business enterprise'
    43; end of Second World War
    44; knowledge-based services
    45–46; meanings of 40–41; new
    managerial class 41; organisation
    and business technique
    45; processes of research,
    development, production and
    marketing 44–45; 'professional
    society' 46; 'quintessence of
    managerialism' 41, 47; rise of
    US managerial capitalism 43;
    'silent revolution' in American
    business 41; social/institutional
    transformation 43; third social
    revolution 45–47; *The Visible Hand*
    42–43
managers, making of 5; Academic
    Approach 11, 12, 13–14; Corporate
    Approach 11, 12, 13; lack of
    structure and progression 12;
    Professional Approach 11, 12–13
Manpower Commission 5
Marris, R. 42
Marxist manager amidst Progressives:
    economic history 96–97; scientific
    management 96, 97–99; socialist
    scientific manager, Polakov as
    103–110; Taylor Society 96; Walter
    Polakov: Taylorist 3–4, 99–103
Marx, K. 47, 56, 104, 105, 106, 109;
    Capital 105
Means, G. C. 3
Ministry of Education Certificate and
    Diploma in Management Studies 10
Ministry of Education (Urwick)
    Committee 8

mixed phase, current (1990s–
    present) 90–91; ambitions of
    professional institutions 86;
    Boston Consulting Group's
    London programme 88; British
    Computer Society's Certificate
    in IS Consultancy Practice 89;
    Certificate in IS Consultancy
    Practice 89; Certified Management
    Consultant (CMC) qualification
    88–89; EDS University's
    Consulting Competency Centre
    87; e-education strategies
    86–87; effects of information
    technology 85; employment of
    digital learning strategies 87;
    initiatives of professional bodies
    88; International Council of
    Management Consulting Institutes
    (ICMCI) 88; Internet, introduction
    and use of 85, 87; marketing and
    sales 87; private training providers
    86–87; specialist IT consultants 86

National Economic Development
    Council 5
National Health Service 7
New Machine 104

off-site training phase (1941–1960s)
    3, 90; Associated Industrial
    Consultants (AIC) 78–79; Bedford
    Work-Study School 76–77, 78;
    'Big Four' 77–78; ICI 76; P-E
    consultants 79; 'Slough Training
    Centre' 78; Urwick Management
    Centre 78
on-the-job training phase (1926–
    1941) 3, 72, 90; advantages 74;
    Bedaux method, skills 73; Bedaux
    training strategy 71; consultants
    from Charles E. Bedaux and
    Company 70; core subjects 71;
    delivery of training 75–76; market
    share 75; problems and weaknesses
    71–72; Production Engineering
    Limited, (P-E) 74–75; staff training
    72–73; and standard of service 74;
    testing regime 73; Urwick, Orr and
    Partners Limited 75

PA Consulting Group 16
Perkin, H. 3, 41, 45, 46
'personal capitalism' 63n40
Person, H. S. 98
Personnel Administration 16, 21, 25
Polakov, Walter N. 3, 96, 97, 111,
117, 118; differential pay rates
106; evolutionary socialist
109–110; and Gantt 101;
intensification of labour 107;
labour theory of value 105; level
of skill or efficiency 106–107;
as Marxist 105; *Mastering
Power Production* 103, 109;
membership of Taylor Society
100–101; New Machine 104;
'Planning Power Plant Work'
102; 'Power Plant Betterment by
Scientific Management' 102; 'The
Progressive Relation between
Efficiency and Consent' 103–104;
'pseudo-democrats' 107; recorded
comments to the Society 103;
scientific management as holistic
practice 101–102; as significant
developer of instrument control
systems 108; socialism 105, 107–
108; as socialist scientific manager
100, 103–110; stunt peddlers 108;
Taylorist 3–4, 99–103; techniques
of modern production 105–106; a
Technocrat 108, 113n27; *Women
under Socialism* 104
Power/Knowledge (Foucault) 53
pre-education and training phase
(1869–1925) 69, 89–90
Privy Council Committee on
Industrial Productivity 7
'Process Analysis Method of
Training' (PAMT) 21
Production Engineering (P-E) 24
Professional Approach 5, 11, 12–13,
29–31

Quail, J. 2

Rizzi, B. 2, 40, 47
Rose, T. G. 19
Rousseau, Jean-Jacques 3

Routledge Focus on Industrial History
1, 4

Scale and Scope (Chandler) 46
'School of Management' 9
scientific management 96; definition
and context 97–99; *a priori*
assumption 98; Progressivism 99
Second Industrial Revolution 44
Servan-Schreiber, J. -J. 3, 41, 44,
45, 51
Seymour, A. H. 21
Slough Training Centre 24, 25, 94n33
specialisation phase (1960s–1990s)
90; Big Four British consultancies
82–83; broadening of consultancy
and movement 82–84; business
appraisals 84; change in corporate
structure, factors 80; consultants
from accounting companies 83;
delivery of services 81; Institute of
Management Consultants (IMC)
80, 84, 85; IT consultants 83–84;
prerequisite of business school
and university education 81–82;
qualification in management
consulting 84; specialisms within
consultancy 84; universities in
Britain 83; work-study 82

Taylor, F. W. 52, 97, 98, 99, 101,
103, 110
Taylorism 3–4
Taylor Society 110–111;
documents 98
Training Within Industry scheme 31

United States Economic
Co-operation Administration 7
Urwick Management Centre 25
'Urwick Report' 30

The Visible Hand (Chandler) 43, 46

Wallace, Mike 117
Whitehead Company 35n47
Whitehead, H. 15, 19, 30, 72
Wren, Daniel 117
Wright Mills, C. 47

For Product Safety Concerns and Information please contact our EU
representative GPSR@taylorandfrancis.com
Taylor & Francis Verlag GmbH, Kaufingerstraße 24, 80331 München, Germany